A Recip

Who would think that serving the Lord is dangerous? We often hear stories of success, but we rarely read about the pain. Dennis unpacks the raw process of burnout that involves disappointment, disillusionment, despair, and betrayal. Yet he offers *insight* to the walking wounded, those approaching burnout, *instruction* for those in burnout mode and are simply going through the motions, and *hope* for those who have checked out because of burnout. His focus on rediscovering a love relationship with God is a key to recovery. This is a must-read for all wounded warriors."

—Senior Pastor Nicholas Seeberger
Church on the Sound, Stony Brook, Long
Island, New York

What a joy it is to wholeheartedly recommend *A Recipe for Fried Christian: Going from Spiritual Burnout to Well-Done Lover of God*. This book is actually a Christian growth manual, first lived out by Dennis Bambino, as he diligently sought to grow as a sincere disciple of Christ. This is a literal journey portrayed in the words of one's life experiences, for you and me to glean much wisdom and truth. The book's title is a witty play on words in Matthew 25:21, "Well done, good and faithful servant." Dennis points out that Jesus chose the words *well done*, not fried. We are all called to be passionate lovers of

Jesus, not burned-out Christians, and learn that empty and unrewarding religious duty is not a substitute for the true calling of abiding in the affection of Jesus as our first Love.

Dennis and his lovely wife, Jackie, regularly attend Dwelling Place Church in Houston, Texas. I know them to be passionate lovers of Jesus and have been privileged to travel with them to distant lands to train and equip the body of Christ. Dennis is an astute teacher with a gift to break down big concepts into bite-sized revelation. I called this a manual because it can be read and prayed over, section by section, as a part of your daily Christian walk. Dennis rightly points us to the preeminence of Christ alone as our destination and reward.

I know you and I are yearning in these last days for the Lord's appearing. My prayer is that we will all hear "well done", and be captured in the rapture and ecstasy of the one whom our soul loves. The journey to our true Love begins now, not just in heaven. It is today that you can hear Him lovingly speak to your heart that you are His beloved.

> Scarcely had I passed by them,
> When I found the one I love.
> I held him and would not let him go.
> (Song of Songs 3:4)

—Randy Needham, Senior Leader
Dwelling Place Church, Ten Cities Movement
Houston, Texas

In the 1980s and 1990s, I had the joy of ministering side by side with Dennis Bambino, recognizing the strong calling on his life, especially to make disciples, but also watching him encounter many serious obstacles along the way. Now, at last, he shares his own story with openness and raw honesty. But he also describes the incredible wholeness He has found in Jesus after enduring deep disappointment and pain. Better still, Dennis also shares what he has learned over the decades—precious, life-changing, ministry-saving truths—so that others can learn from his experiences. You will find this book to be as practical as it is inspirational. As you read you may even recognize your own story.

—Dr. Michael L. Brown, host, the *Line of Fire* broadcast, author of *Jezebel's War with America*

As a pastoral counselor for over thirty-five years, it is refreshing to see one courageous enough to share, with heartfelt authenticity, the struggles he faced in processing his pain and pushing through to life-changing spiritual victory. Unfortunately, there are many believers, and in too many cases leaders, who settle for far less than the real deal. The author shows us, through his gut wrenching failures and losses, that we too can come out of multiple crisis situations, trials, and tribulations, if we hold tightly to the Lord and yield to His Holy Spirit leading us into greater levels of freedom and liberty.

Using his own life experiences, the author provides encouragement to other believers in how to pursue God in spite of being betrayed, spiritually trounced, and crushed. He offers a pattern, guiding us through the process he experienced in his journey to wholeness, security, and greater intimacy with God. His story provides wisdom and insights, which cannot be learned without going through the furnace of affliction. I highly recommend this book. It is for all who truly desire to follow the Lord, no matter the cost.

—Rev. Ivan Doxtator, MSW
CEO—First Nations Restoration Ministries

Experience the rich and intense presence of God as Dennis invites us into his raw and real journey with transparency and vulnerability. You will be impacted, undone, and empowered. For all those who have been hurt by fellow believers or have hurt others inadvertently, this book is a must-read. It gives insight into the spiritual and emotional forces that come into play when there has been betrayal, offense, or misunderstanding. This book is pithy and vital for growth and strength as we experience re-formation accomplished by Holy Spirit.

Dennis Bambino is a friend of the Great Shepherd and a friend of the sheep. He is a prophetic teacher, a living epistle, and an apostolic general.

—Rev. Tom and Barbara Mercier
Board Chairmen, "Arise! Ukraine Ministries"

In his book, Dennis Bambino takes us through his time of being broken and bloodied and left on the side of the road. He shares his story with the kind of gut-wrenching honesty that will encourage anyone reading it to examine self, motives, and choices. This book is overdue for many Christians who were raised up to put on a "happy face" and just keep going no matter what happens. I believe Dennis's story and his honest and insightful revelations gained through years of experiences will help bring freedom to others. Dennis says it beautifully: *"To move forward today, into your tomorrows, you must resolve your yesterdays."*

If you have ever been betrayed, wounded or hurt by those you trusted, this book will help set you free! We will be adding it to our resource list for those in need.

—Linda Doxtator, PhD, LPC, LCPC
Clinical Director, First Nations Restoration Ministries

This book is a treasure brought from the back of Dennis' painful experiences. The deep honesty in sharing what the Lord taught him through his life journey is a rare gift to the body of Christ to learn from. We fully endorse this book. We would say that by receiving this message, you will save yourself from losing a lot of time, wasting a lot of energy, and going in the wrong direction.
May you become who the Lord has called you to be.

—Rev. Guine and Lisa Anderson
Founders, Harvest Now Inc.

Dennis shares the lessons he learned as he was becoming "well done" clearly and concisely. This is a great text to read if you think you might be burning out, or would like to avoid burn out. In my forty years of providing guidance to leaders, I am convinced that leaders like Dennis and me are going to get fried a bit, and some of us will get burned, but that can lead to resurrection. Burnout is not just a product of being in a tough place. It happens when you isolate, fail to heed wise counsel, and cling to "proven methods of success," when God may be directing us down a different path. I knew Dennis when he was in constant motion. His love of God became love of accomplishment, and he was drawn to models and examples that sometimes burned out his followers. He writes how God forced him to go from constant activity to the spiritual discipline of solitude. Instead of rushing through the day, he is mindful of nature, love, and beauty, with gratitude.

Most of all, this is a book about redemption. In soul-crushing circumstances, God's magnificent grace shows up, and He reveals something new about His character, who we are, and what He has called us to be. Dennis wrote, *"It's not what I've done but who I've become that pleases the Lord the most. 'Lord, I surrender to being transformed by You.'"* I will be rereading this book, and recommending it to my clients. I look forward to the next one, Dennis.

—Paul VanValin, PhD. is the founder and president of Eden Counseling and Consulting in Norfolk, Virginia. He is licensed in Virginia to practice clinical psychology. Paul provides coaching and consulting, and assessments for leaders and teams, through VanValin Assessment and Consultation, LLC. He is a certified coach in PRO-D Comprehensive Assessment, a leadership assessment, and Prepare/Enrich, a marriage enrichment assessment.

He is the author of *Win Every Argument, Win Every Heart: A Leader's Guide to Effective Communication.*

What an honor and joy for me to write an endorsement for Apostle Dennis Bambino. If anyone, he is truly well experienced to write about this topic. He has planted churches, pastored churches, and overseen networks. With this valuable experience, this book will bring you into a journey of understanding the continuously changing dynamics of life as a leader. I'm so deeply touched by his transparency in this book. It will help leaders like me to know that transparency brings great safety and empowerment. I'm thankful that Dennis is well able to speak into the orphan heart to allow the sons in hiding to arise.

This is a book every scared, burned out, broken leader needs to read. This is a navigation system of truths that will enable all who long to lead like Christ to arise and become truly the leader they were meant to be. Thank you for this very deep and truthful story. I'm confident it will allow leaders to arise into higher confidence of who they were meant to become.

—Apostle David McDonald
North Palm Global
HIM Apostolic Ambassador

A Recipe for Fried Christian

*Going from Spiritual Burnout
to Well-Done Lover of God*

Dennis C. Bambino

XULON PRESS

Xulon Press
2301 Lucien Way #415
Maitland, FL 32751
407.339.4217
www.xulonpress.com

© 2020 by Dennis C. Bambino

All rights reserved solely by the author. The author guarantees all contents are original and do not infringe upon the legal rights of any other person or work. No part of this book may be reproduced in any form without the permission of the author. The views expressed in this book are not necessarily those of the publisher.

Unless otherwise indicated, Scripture quotations taken from the Holy Bible, New International Version (NIV). Copyright © 1973, 1978, 1984, 2011 by Biblica, Inc.™. Used by permission. All rights reserved.

Paperback ISBN-13: 978-1-6628-0292-8
Ebook ISBN-13: 978-1-6628-0293-5

Dedication

To all those wounded warriors who have found themselves in the cave of Adullam—fried—in distress, in debt, and disconnected: "He who is the glory of Israel will come to Adullam" (Mic. 1:15). He will turn your refuge into a stronghold and your tomb into a womb. The Son of David will rebirth you, lead you forth in victory, and re-create you into a lavish lover and a worshiping warrior.

To my rescuer, the Lord Jesus Christ: Your love was deeper than my darkness, more healing than my hurt, more powerful than my pain, and more faithful than my failures. Your tender mercies and loving-kindness transformed me from the inside out.

To my wife, Jackie: You faithfully stood by my side and continued to love me when I had nothing to give you.

To my daughters and sons-in-love: You never stopped loving me.

To my very special friends Joe and Katie, Kathy, Lou and Nilda, Darlene and Jeff, Yvette and Bob, and Barbara: Like Jesus, all of you stuck closer than a brother. You believed the Lord for me and believed in me when I couldn't.

To Bishop Joseph Mattera whose friendship and counsel, as my overseer, continually guided and strengthened me.

Contents

Praise for *A Recipe for Fried Christian* i
Dedication xi
Foreword by Bishop Joseph Mattera xvii
Introduction: Well-Done—Not Fried—
Good And Faithful Servant xxi

Part One: How to Become a Fried Christian 1

1: My Story, Part I—From Freedom to Fried 3
   My Heart 3
   New Beginnings 3
      Out of Traditional Religion | Birth Pangs |
      Birth of the Call | Freedom | Paternal Rejection
   The Call Crystallized 7
   Visions And Dreams 8
   Mismatched Transition 9
      The Missing Father Factor| Constant Conflict |
      Stress Cracks
   Beneath The Coming Earthquake 14
      The Tipping Point | Betrayed and Exiled
   Emotional Devastation 17
      Self-condemnation | Violent Assault | Rejection |
      Identity Destruction | Robbed at Gunpoint |
      Heartbroken | Injustice
   Pushing Past The Pain 20

A Recipe for Fried Christian

    Free Fall Into Darkness 21
        Fried | Numb | Depressed | Deserted by God | Alone |
        Betrayal Turned Inward | Failure | Court-martialed |
        No Sure Foundation
    It's Over. I Quit! 26
        To Be Continued

2: A Recipe For Fried Christian—
    How To Become Fried 29
    No One Wants To Be Fried 29
    The Recipe 30
        The Overall Process | The Process: Time and Pressure |
        Very Important Note
    The Seven Deadly Ingredients......................32
        Ingredient 1: A Tender Or A Tough Christian
        Ingredient 2: The Batter
        Ingredient 3: A Full Cup Of Crushed Spirit
        Ingredient 4: A Pound Of Principles From The Pit
        Ingredient 5: A Container Of Corrupted Common Sense
        Ingredient 6: Ten Pints Of Prideful Persistence
        Ingredient 7: A Large Ladle Of Lethal Lies
    Conflict In The Kitchen...........................46
    The Crucible Of Critical Crisis......................47
    Don't Despair....................................48

Part Two: How to Become a
              Well-Done Lover of God 49

3: My Story, Part II—From Fried to Well-Done 53
    What Happened Next............................53
        He Wrapped Me | The Honeymoon |
        How Great Thou Art
    New Roots 56
        Converted to Living Inside Out | Dismantled Errant
        Principles | The One Thing | Joy | Rest | Transformation
    The Challenges...................................61
        Love your enemies | The Ongoing Battles
    My Story Is Not Over 63

Going from Spiritual Burnout to Well-Done Lover of God

The Continuing Process | Confident and Convinced

4: How to Become a Well-Done Lover of God 65
    Everybody Wants To Finish Well 65
    The Purposes, Processes, And Places
    For Becoming Well Done 66
        Love: The Key Ingredient
    The Processes For Becoming Well-Done 68
        Process 1: From Trash To Transformation
        Process 2: From Reduction To Production
        Process 3: From Information To Revelation;
            From Conflicted to Convinced
        Process 4: From Forgiven To Forgiving
            And Beyond
        Process 5: From Reorientation To
            Re-Formation And Re-Definition
        Process 6: From Laborer To Lover
        Process 7: From Hurt To Healing
        Process 8: From Failure To Formation
        Process 9: Fire For Refining
        Process 10: The Father Factor: Orphan To Son
    The Places For Becoming Well-Done 107
    Ten Powerful Purposes Of Separation 111
        The Secret Place | Separation
        1. Separation Develops Maturation.
        2. Separation For Purification Prepares
           Us For Intercession.
        3. Separation Becomes The Battleground For
           Confrontation That Results In Domination.
        4. Separation Facilitates Rejuvenation.
        5. Separation Is The Environment
           Of Dedication That Brings Visitation.
        6. Separation Births Revelation.
        7. Separation Produces Declaration.
        8. Separation Marks Us With Identification.
        9. Separation Positions Us For Impartation.
        10. Separation Releases Evangelization.

5: Well-Done Christian Nuggets: Fast Food for Christians on the Run to Becoming Well-Done .. 125
    Quick Principles and Prayers........................ 125
    More Nuggets for the Hungry...................... 127

6: Well-Done Christian Cordon Bleu: Serving the Best to a Hungry World 135
    The End Purposes Of The Father 135
    Serving Ourselves To The World.................... 135
  Testimonies Of His Transforming Power............136
    Testimony 1: From Tragedy to Triumph
    Testimony 2: From Retired to Refired

7: An Invitation to Become a Well-Done Lover of God 143
  Help! I'm Fried!.................................143
    To Surrender | To Separate | To Serve | To Stand

Closing Prayer 149

About The Author 151

Foreword

Dennis Bambino has written a very important book! In it he tells the story of how he as a Christian leader, can effectively minister under an anointing while all the while neglecting his inner person. His story is important because this is a common issue for all spiritual leaders, especially those with high demand upon them, such as a pastor.

With an amazing ability to articulate his brokenness, Dennis teaches us how God used outside pressure and even a church-related crisis to get through to him. Consequently, God is more interested in our deep relationship with Him than He is with mere outward forms, behavior, and ministry. God has truly called us to "inside-out leadership" as opposed to "outside-in leadership."

Jesus also addressed this when He called out the religious leaders of His day for being whitewashed tombs, who appeared to men to be righteousness but inside were full of dead men's bones and everything unclean. (See Matt. 23)

I have heard Dennis tell his story numerous times, and every time I hear it, I get fresh insight related to my own condition, which challenges me to become more self-aware. I also resonate with him because several times in my life in the past two decades, I felt that I was doing damage to my soul and was perilously close to minor burnout due to my intense schedule. I have also personally walked with Dennis and his lovely wife Jackie through some of their darkest times related to church ministry, so his journey is very real to me.

After reading this book you will have to come to the conclusion that it ultimately profits us nothing if we "win the world but forfeit our soul."

My hope is that every pastor, spiritual leader, and serious Christ follower use this book as a tool to truly examine their life in the light of His Word and presence; that this work will be used to bring restoration to thousands of burned out servants of Christ. My desire is for this work to become a catalyst for lonely leaders to get connected to smaller clusters of leaders for mutual accountability and benefit. I believe this book can be an amazing resource for Bible schools, seminaries, and churches and can be used in small group studies as well as retreats.

May Dennis's brokenness result in the healing and wholeness of many. May his "mess" become a "message" of healing and hope for other burned out fellow travelers. May it result in many of us having honest conversations with ourselves, our spouses, and associates related to the true condition of our souls. May the great wounded Healer, Jesus Christ, highlight the thoughts and concepts conveyed that are relevant to our condition so that He can purge from us all hypocrisy and uncleanness. By His wounds may we be healed.

—Bishop Joseph Mattera
National convener of United States Coalition of Apostolic leaders

Introduction

Well-Done—Not Fried—
Good And Faithful Servant

Experiences in life can be cruel and destructive. Many of us have suffered from situations that were out of our control: rejection, betrayal, hatred, violence against our bodies and souls, as well as accusations and misunderstandings that have beaten us and left us for dead. Abandoned and alone, we have found ourselves in places of deep discouragement, depression, and hopelessness. Fried, burned out, cooked, shot, finished, done! These words all describe people who, having made every effort to save themselves and change threatening situations, have expended all their energies and find themselves completely exhausted and at the end of themselves. Now, in little more than a vegetative state, they wallow in what has been called "the dark night of the soul," waiting for something or someone to save them.

I have been there, and this is my story. In these pages, I share where I have been, how I got there, how the Lord renewed me, and what I learned along the way. I have attempted to tell my story, not as a defense of myself, nor in disregard of what others went through and felt during these events, but as an honest reflection of my journey, with all its both ugly and beautiful experiences. It has taken years for me to unpack the events that radically changed my life:

> To be secure enough in God's love to not be afraid to be honest with myself and others;
>
> To be able to put words to my pain;
>
> To sort out my soul, exhuming all its buried emotions and thoughts;
>
> To separate truth from the lies and deceptions I came to believe;
>
> To be able to face my failings and sin without condemnation;
>
> To ask for forgiveness, to be forgiven, and to forgive;
>
> To be healed in broken relationships;
>
> To come to know the Lord of love and learn to love myself, others, and even my enemies;
>
> To be re-created in my identity; and

To have my destiny reignited.

I could not have written this book any sooner, although I tried. There were experiences I still needed to have and processes I still needed to go through. The Lord is the real author, and I knew He was still writing *His* book. He told me, *You are not worth more to anyone because you have written a book, but you are worth more to everyone if My book is written in you.* He has now released me to write His book about my story. The title of this book is a play on words from Matthew 25:21, where the Lord says, "Well done, good and faithful servant." He wants all of us to stand before Him "well-done," not fried and burned out. To tell my story, I have used the analogy of cooking chicken, exchanging *Christian* for *chicken,* and taking the Christian from "fried" to "well-done."

Chapter One, "My Story Part I—From Freedom to Fried," includes the experiences leading up to my becoming fried, as well as the effects those experiences had on me.

Chapter Two, "A Recipe for Fried Christian," details the lessons I learned on how to become fried.

In Chapter Three, "My Story, Part II—From Fried to Freedom," I share the journey of how the Lord revolutionized my life.

The fourth chapter, "How to Become a Well-Done Lover of God." dives into the purposes, processes, and places the Lord uses to produce a well-done Christian.

Chapter Five, "Well-Done Christian Nuggets," offers some fast-food practical tips for staying healthy and well-done.

Chapter Six, "Well-Done Christian Cordon Bleu" highlights a couple of testimonies of how the Lord served me, well-done, to others.

And finally, Chapter Seven, "An Invitation to Become a Well-Done Lover of God," issues a call to surrender to the Lord's processes and become the well-done lover He has destined you to be.

Though I am still a work in progress, it is my desire that what I have experienced will encourage you, bring you hope, and light a path that will enable you to walk out of darkness and the pain of the past. I hope the lessons I have learned will help you avoid the pitfalls of becoming fried and lead you into the fullness of a love relationship with the Lord.

No matter how fried you've become or how hopeless the situation looks, there is Someone who loves you, who will redeem what the enemy has meant for evil, heal you, and cause you to become the person He created you to be. He does the "doing" until you are well-done. His name is Jesus. He did it for me, and He will do it for you.

Part One

How to Become a
Fried Christian

Therefore everyone who hears these words of mine and puts them into practice is like a wise man who built his house on the rock. The rain came down, the streams rose, and the wind blew and beat against that house; yet it did not fall, because it had its foundation on the rock. But everyone who hears these words of mine and does not put them into practice is like a foolish man who built his house on sand. The rain came down, the streams rose, and the winds blew and beat against that house, and it fell with a great crash.
(Matt. 7:24–27)

There is a way that seems right to a man, but in the end it leads to death. (Prov. 14:12)

I will instruct you and teach you in the way you should go;
    I will counsel you and watch over you.
Do not be like the horse or the mule,
    which have no understanding but must be controlled by bit and bridal
    or they will not come to you.

(Ps. 32:8-9)

Chapter One

My Story, Part I— From Freedom to Fried

MY HEART

As I begin my story, I want to be as transparent as possible so that you can come to understand, as I have, all that I experienced when my heart was broken and my visions and dreams were shattered. This part of my story took me from being freed *to* serve the Lord to being fried *from* serving the Lord.

NEW BEGINNINGS

I was swept into God's kingdom during the charismatic renewal in the early 1970s. It was a very exciting time. Multitudes were coming out of traditional religion and moving into a personal relationship with the Lord Jesus Christ. Thousands gathered in fields to praise the Lord, churches were filled with charismatic prayer and healing meetings, house meetings erupted all around, and signs, wonders, and miracles were commonplace. It was also a chaotic time. People discovered a new freedom in Christ but didn't know what to do with it. Character lagged far behind the use of the gifts of the Holy Spirit. There were to few mature spiritual fathers to teach, train, and correct young and immature converts. Many casualties resulted over the next several decades as the church tried to find its way and develop roots in truth.

Out of Traditional Religion

What I was learning in the Word and experiencing as a new believer conflicted with many things I had always believed and practiced in my traditional denomination. At the end of a one-on-one conference with the pastor of my church over the Word of God versus the church's teaching, I was invited to leave the church. Not knowing where to go, my wife and I decided to stay home on Sundays and have church as a family. It was a precious time of growth for us. We learned how to pray for one another, saw our children baptized in the Holy Spirit, and worshiped the Lord as a family. After one year, we were joined by many other people looking for a place to go on Sundays. Our home meetings grew and grew. We eventually maxed out all of our houses, rented facilities, and then bought a building. We had become a church.

Birth Pangs

These times sparked a desire in me to serve the Lord for the rest of my life. I told the Lord I wanted to be like

Paul and take the gospel to the ends of the earth. My previous ambition to become successful in business shriveled up and died. The only way I could justify staying in business was to use every opportunity in it to share the Lord, which I did. In fact, I led many people to Christ in my office and on business trips. One man from the factory came to the Lord and got delivered on the conference room table! The last I heard, he was pastoring in the Bronx. Another associate dramatically came to the Lord after two years of witnessing to him. He is now pastoring in Alabama.

The president of the company warned me, with his finger in my face, that if I continued to proselytize on company time and property, I would be fired. The Lord, however, made it clear to me that He was the one who had put me in that position and no one could remove me from it. Following that word, I began taking a half dozen young converts off premises at lunchtime to share the Word with them. Several months later, our company was sold, the president was replaced, and I was given a promotion.

Birth of the Call

I knew the Lord was with me, and I was hungry for training in the Word. During my nine years in business, I went anywhere and did everything I could to receive biblical training from conferences, courses, and self-study. My frustration with staying in business became unbearable, despite the fact that the Lord prospered me—promoting me to vice president and increasing my income to six figures.

Then, while I was on a family vacation to Spain and Switzerland, God dramatically called me to follow Him. He said, *"Love takes the plunge."* With sobbing acceptance, I knew I was to trust Him with everything: my family, my finances, and my future. But it didn't make sense; it wasn't logical. I returned from the trip, and my call was confirmed by elder Christians. The Lord didn't tell me what His plan was, how it was going to work, or how I would support my family. Nonetheless, I knew what I needed to do first: resign my position as vice president—with its income, benefits, and future. So I did it. I took the plunge. (It's a great testimony. I would love to share all the details with you someday about the call and how He totally provided for me and my family.)

Freedom

I felt as though I had been shot out of a cannon, set free to be all that He called me to be. That was it for me. It was now full speed ahead. I was all in, no turning back.

Paternal Rejection

The cost of following Jesus quickly mounted. I was amazed that most people did not understand the decision I made. Friends and family thought I was being too radical. My father, in particular, was very angry and disappointed in me. He disowned me for leaving the religion he had raised me in and for forsaking my career, accusing me in front of my children of choosing to "shoot marbles" with the rest of my life. I was livid with him for demeaning me in front of my children and deeply wounded by his rejection. Consequently, we didn't have much of a relationship for the next ten years. Disappointed and dismayed at the lack of affirmation from others and wounded by my father's rejection, I had to trust fully in my experience with the Lord when He called me.

God is faithful, and two years before my father passed away, he accepted the Lord, publicly acknowledged me as a "good son," and blessed me. While that brought a sense of closure, I still did not feel totally confirmed in my calling.

THE CALL CRYSTALLIZED

Through a trusted minister, the Lord prophetically reiterated I should "take the plunge" and directed me to attend Christ for the Nations Institute of Biblical Studies (CFNIBS) for one year. At forty years old, I couldn't understand why the Lord was putting me with young adults, studying things I had already learned on my own. He then gave me a vision of a golf ball without a cover, exposing rubber bands sticking out all over. He told me He had to take care of all the loose ends and then wrap me with a hard cover because He was going to send me into difficult places around the world. Amazingly, the Lord provided all of my family's needs for that entire year of study.

At the end of that year, I was offered a position at the school as an instructor and the director of student ministries. I created and taught courses, and I was involved in discipleship training and missionary outreach, where I led students into the field locally and internationally. I called it Christian Shangri-la. For five-and-a-half years,

I flowed in my gifts and felt as if this was what I was created for. The students in attendance paid to be there, setting aside their lives to be equipped, discipled, and sent out on their assignments. They easily came under authority and were willing to be trained and disciplined in their studies, character, and habits. I was ministering to students who were on fire for the Lord and wanted to do His will at any cost. They were hungry for everything I had to give them.

The fruit from that time at CFNIBS was abundant. This is where my calling was crystallized: make disciples in the character of Christ, equip them for works of service, send them into the world to spread the gospel, build the kingdom of God, and prepare the body of Christ for Jesus's second coming.

VISIONS AND DREAMS

During this time, the Lord was giving me dreams, visions, and many revelations from His Word. One important revelation was about Ezekiel's vision of a valley of dry bones coming together and being raised up as a great and mighty army. He gave me insight as to why the bones were dry and revealed that the application was for the church today. In this revelation, the Lord showed me the process He would use to bring about the unity of the body of Christ and make it a mighty army. He detailed what each phase in the vision meant. I saw people coming together regionally and nationally to be the "one church," around an apostolic order raised up with all its parts strategically connected as compassion covered the entire body. This army became a force in the earth, destroying the works of the enemy, releasing captive souls, and establishing the kingdom of God.

Zeal for my calling and the many dreams, visions, and revelations from the Word emboldened my preaching and teaching. Being militant in my approach to making disciples was acceptable at CFNIBS. At the school, we understood we were training an army. The urgency that permeated my ministry was fueled by visions of souls being lost every day, understanding that time was running out, Jesus was coming soon, and we needed to get the job done. I was dedicated to making disciples who made disciples. I was convinced this was Jesus's primary command and method to evangelize the world.

Oddly enough, I was perceived by students as having two contrasting sides. In public, they likened me to a drill sergeant. They called me "Bambo," a commander who trained soldiers and led the charge into battle. In private one-on-one conversations, or in counseling or mentoring situations, they experienced me as a father. I opted to be more of the former and to avoid the latter.

MISMATCHED TRANSITION

People began gathering to me and wanted me to start a church, but I couldn't do that while an instructor at the school. It would have been perceived as a conflict of interest. So when CFNIBS closed, I immediately (in hindsight, presumptively) started a church. However, I knew I wasn't called to be a pastor. Evangelist, yes. Teacher, probably. But pastor? I knew I wasn't a pastor. I was confident that I was called to teach and train and go to the nations, but I was unsure about staying home and caring for the sheep. Consequently, when I started the church, I partnered with a man who had a pastoral call and set him in as pastor. It didn't work. The people insisted on calling me "Pastor" and expected me to perform as one. Their expectations and my hesitation to actually pastor created ongoing conflict within me and in the church.

I brought my vision, dreams, methodology, and a full boatload of zeal into the local church setting. That was like putting the Pentagon in charge of the Department of Education. The majority of the people didn't want a drill sergeant or a commander leading them into battle; they just wanted to be cared for and have their felt needs met. With many people shopping churches to find the programs they wanted, I allowed programs to be installed that didn't fit my vision. This created a church with multiple visions pulling against one another, ultimately resulting in division.

The Missing Father Factor

People wanted me to be more of the father they needed, but I didn't feel called or equipped to be a father at that time. I did not want to try to be someone I wasn't, and at the same time, I did not want to neglect the call to make disciples and go to the nations. I struggled to take on the identity of a spiritual father when I didn't know what a spiritual father looked like. I didn't have one, but I knew I needed one. Without that relationship, I felt like an orphan. I asked the Lord many times to give me a spiritual father but got no answer. I asked several mature men I admired to be my spiritual father and received only blank stares in response.

On a six-day retreat, alone with the Lord, He revealed to me that He was my spiritual Father, and I was His son. It was revelatory. I felt deeply transformed and could not wait to share my newfound realization. However, on the way home, an apostolic minister called and asked me to partner with him to install a vision he had for the region. His vision resonated with so many of my visions that I quickly got involved and was soon very busy. Sadly, the revelation of my sonship and the fatherhood of God never had a chance to root and thus quickly faded.

Constant Conflict

Throughout the time I was a pastor, I constantly battled contrary mind-sets, traditions, religious formats, and other visions and hidden agendas that conflicted with what I believed the church should be. It was like herding cats, building sand castles on an incoming tide, and spinning plates. In complete contrast to how I felt when teaching the students at CFNIBS, I now felt as though I was trying to get people to do things they didn't want to do, to go places they didn't want to go, and to become something they didn't want to become. These conflicts kept tension in the church at a consistently high level.

Being "purpose driven" was a popular concept at the time. That idea fueled the push to realize my vision for the church, despite resistance. We adopted church-growth models, prayer, and evangelistic programs in an attempt to equip the church, multiply, and go into the world with the gospel. Small groups, or cells, seemed to offer a solution for both pastoring and training; thus, training small-group leaders became our discipleship program. Small-group leaders were trained to care for the sheep, to be evangelistic, and to multiply. But in reality, there was very little multiplication. People wanted to stay in the same groups. As a result, we experienced more groups dying than groups being born.

Pastors were ordained and deacons licensed to build the leadership base of the church. These were the people closest to me, most of them my spiritual sons and daughters. I trusted them to care for the sheep and protect the vision of the church. They manned the pulpit when I traveled and directly interacted with the people and other leaders of the church. I put them between me and the congregation. They were my face to the people. This freed me to work in the region as well as internationally.

A trip to Bogotá, Colombia, introduced me to a cell-church concept called G-12, or groups of twelve. The mother church there was experiencing explosive multiplication, and the concept was being adopted around the world by veteran leaders who were converting their churches from merely having small groups to being a cell church. Midweek services were canceled, and everyone in the church was placed in a cell. Everyone in the cell was considered a soul-winner and a future cell leader. Leaders trained their people to win souls, care for them, disciple them, and multiply their cells within a short period of time.

We adopted the G-12 program and became a cell church. Over a period of six months, all our leaders were trained in the "principle of twelve," and the new vision for the church was installed. The pressure to perform, however, was more than most people wanted to commit to. Not long after installing the program, the church experienced an exodus of leaders and sheep, and lost people to the tune of −35 percent.

During all this time, I was ministering in the nations at conferences and evangelistic crusades. In my local region, great initiatives were started—several of which I spearheaded—aimed at bringing unity among the churches for the purpose of evangelizing the region. There were many times these ministry activities took me out of the church and the pulpit, sometimes for weeks at a time.

Stress Cracks

The demands of ministry became overwhelming. Moving things forward, keeping things together, and putting out fires became a nonstop, 24/7 job. While it was my heart's desire to release people, I found myself becoming more and more controlling in order to keep the vision moving forward. Not infrequently, I was accused of being a micromanager. My prayer life dwindled. My time in the Word was now used to generate the next "amazing" message.

My marriage suffered from the stress. For years, I had put ministry before my marriage and family. At one point, my wife rightly accused me of the ministry being my mistress. My children had suffered the loss of my attention or presence at different times as they grew up. Now, years later, I was spending precious little time with my married children and grandchildren. With them now living a thousand miles away, coupled with the demands on my life, I was cut off from the only fun I had ever allowed myself. I was stuck in a cycle where there was no time to rest; there was too much to do. Any enjoyment I had once experienced in ministry was now replaced with loneliness, anger, and fatigue.

My relationship with the core team became more and more distant. Communications were difficult and strained. Our time together was relegated to solving problems. Honest, transparent sharing of our hearts no longer existed. Spending time together over a meal, laughing, fellowshipping, and just enjoying one another as we once did ceased to exist.

All I have just shared with you was obviously fertile ground for big trouble.

BENEATH THE COMING EARTHQUAKE

Choosing leaders to surround you and carry out the vision of the house is more than just a science or an art. It's spiritual. It's not about choosing talented, gifted, and called men and women to fill a position in the organization. It has more to do with whether or not they have your heart, hold your visions and dreams as their own, cover your back, and even more, whether their motive to be in leadership is pure. It has to do with being united in primary core values, absolute agreement in fundamental truths of the Word of God, being one in spirit and the willingness to work together, pray together, pay the price, and walk together on the same path to get to a God-ordained end goal.

These leaders are spiritually revealed and spiritually confirmed. Nevertheless, the leaders the Lord has for us to walk with must be tested by time, come forth under pressure, and be found faithful through a crisis. Every leader knows there are people who the Lord has sent to stand beside them as armor bearers and who eventually become their spiritual sons and daughters, even as Joshua was to Moses and Jonathan was to David. These have a covenantal heart connection with you, will stand by your side, and if necessary, take a bullet for you.

Then there are those who find their way into leadership and overtly or covertly covet your pulpit, position, and power without paying the price to get it themselves. They will feign support for a time with the ultimate intention of using the opportunities you give them to advance their own agendas. Though they look good on paper and the possibilities of synergism with you is great, even though you can't put your finger on it, something in your gut tells you it's not a good fit and something is not right. It is the spiritual gift of intuition, telling you what you cannot know by reason, intellect, or natural observation.

In my cadre of leaders, there were those that I knew were my spiritual sons and daughters, those that were faithful servants, and those that my spirit had reservations about. I allowed all of them to continue in leadership and grow in influence with the people. Unfortunately, with those that I had reservations about, I foolishly ignored my intuition and believed we could resolve differences as we worked together. Blowing stop signs, I kept moving forward, taking no action to confront differences and correct them. I tolerated the gap that was developing in vision and approaches to ministry. It would only be a matter of time before subterranean differences would build up pressure, suddenly move, and create a devastating earthquake.

The Tipping Point

It is said that the captain of the ship often sets up the right circumstances for a mutiny. I certainly did that. Everyone knew I was unrelenting in my vision and the direction of the church—and that I was at odds with other visions that had taken root in the church. The pressure I put on the people to perform under the programs was crushing the congregation. My frustration and anger with the increasing battle against opposing visions and leaders gave ammunition to attack my character. My succession plan pointed to certain sons and daughters and exasperated others who had aspirations to move up when I moved out. However, I made it clear I had no intentions of moving out nor relinquishing oversight of the church.

It seemed the tipping point had been reached. I can only surmise that many thought it was now time to "save the ship," remove me, and for others to take charge and chart a new course. On what I call "D Day," taking opportunity from my absence, the entire congregation was presented with the new leadership.

Betrayed and Exiled

I felt ambushed. For me, it was a surprise attack, a Pearl Harbor. I should have seen it coming. But I was too blinded by my own agendas, too busy to stop and see what was really going on, too disconnected from people to hear what they had to say, and too afraid to believe my intuitions were correct. Unfortunately, due to my disconnect from people and their fear of approaching me, no one ever came to me personally, one-on-one, face-to-face, to share their grievances with me. It seemed there had never been a real friend to come to me and wound me with the truth.

Like Joseph, conspired against by his own brothers to kill him and his dream, beaten and left for dead, I was deeply wounded, shocked, confused, angry, and disoriented. "This couldn't be happening to me." I felt my trust was violated. I felt like I was betrayed by some of my closest friends and leaders. It seemed to me that a trial had taken place without my presence, with no one to defend me and no advocate to plead my case. I was never specifically confronted with the charges, only the verdict. I was given one option: to leave. I would not be honored as the founding elder or be in a position of apostolic oversight. By that time, minds had been made up, plans had been formed, and too many suns had set on too many piled-up offenses, making reconciliation seem an impossibility. Nevertheless, we pursued months of professional intervention to no avail. I could relate to Jesus during His arrest and trials: betrayed by his own, conspired against in private, kissed in public, and then abandoned by His closest friends.

With all possible efforts to avoid a split expended, a "divorce agreement" was signed. I then blessed the congregation in a public service and left.

EMOTIONAL DEVASTATION

Whether in marriage, ministry, or business, betrayal is emotionally devastating. It has taken me years to summon the courage to exhume buried emotions and to put words to the pain I experienced during that time. I share them with you in the hope that they will help you to process your own devastating experiences.

Self-condemnation

I was really down on myself, beating myself up for lacking the discernment needed to see what was happening and the courage to correct it. I concluded that I had been complacent in confronting fundamental differences. What I did see, I ignored. Fearing the worst, I barreled through stop signs in my attempt to move ahead.

Violent Assault

The experience was violent. The divorce left me feeling torn apart. Suddenly a part of me was missing. Like in an abortion, spiritual sons and daughters were ripped from me. The sudden death of relationships with friends, co-laborers, and family members was deeply painful. My dreams and visions were torn apart right before my eyes. Sorrow and grief for all I was losing welled up inside me.

Rejection

The pain of rejection is difficult to experience under any circumstances, but when it comes from people you've loved and looked to for acceptance, it is almost unbearable. The message was very clear to me: I didn't measure up. Though I chose to love them, they chose not to love me in return. I'd been dropped from the team.

Worse than that, I felt driven out of the family, as if they were clearly saying, "We no longer want a relationship with you." The acceptance of the few remaining people provided a bit of Novocaine, but it didn't numb the brunt of the pain.

Identity Destruction

My identity was under mortal assault. There was no acknowledgment or thanks for any good done, no intent to help me correct my errors, and no effort to preserve or restore me. It became apparent that a demonic plot lay behind all the rhetoric, not just to remove me, but to totally destroy me, stripping me of identity and self-worth. As a father and founder of the church, I felt disrespected. As a minister, the threat of harming my reputation hung heavy over my head. *What are all the local and international leaders and pastors going to think of me?* I wondered. As a man, I experienced guilt and shame. I felt like David, stripped of being king by his own son Absalom, exiled, expelled, and driven out of the ministry that had become my identity.

Robbed at Gunpoint

That's how it felt. I was robbed of any joy I had once experienced in ministry. Robbed of the hope of seeing my dreams and visions come to pass. Robbed of the confidence of doing what I thought the Lord told me to do. Robbed of my ability to enjoy the blessings the Lord had given me in my wife, family, and grandchildren. I had been robbed of my trust in other people. While the events triggered the robbery, I was yet to discover the true thief.

Heartbroken

Beneath my best efforts to deny my feelings and press on, I was heartbroken. While I never physically cried, my heart overflowed with pain and tears. My hopes were not just deferred—they were crushed. My sick heart struggled with hopelessness.

Injustice

I was angry over the injustice of not having a fair trial. I wanted vindication, and I wanted those who had wronged me to recognize their wrong. In reality, they walked away feeling righteous, while I crawled away feeling condemned.

PUSHING PAST THE PAIN

Carrying these mostly unresolved burdens, I pushed past the pain, quickly collecting the few who stayed with me, appointed leaders, and started to plant house churches. As the house churches multiplied, I repeated my pattern and set in new pastors to oversee and care for the sheep.

My dream of unity in our region and my calling to make disciples moved me to start a regional Bible school. Several pastors caught the vision and enthusiastically jumped on board. The school quickly grew to over sixty students in three locations around the region.

Additionally, "Saturday Seminars for Service," as they were called, were well attended. However, I could not secure a commitment from other teachers to come on board, and I soon found myself teaching all the courses in all the locations. The burden became overwhelming, and I eventually had to shut the school down. Another dream died.

Simultaneously, a pastor of the house churches went rogue. I was forced to shut down the house churches, and as much as possible, place the sheep in other churches.

FREE FALL INTO DARKNESS

Fried

That was it. I was done, finished, burned out, fried. For the past several years, ever since the first crash, I had thrashed and desperately tried to save myself, pushing through the pain, making every effort to get up and keep going. Now I found myself completely and utterly exhausted in every way—physically, emotionally, mentally, and spiritually. I was spent and empty. This was the beginning of a free fall into a very dark and lonely place. I felt like Jonah, swallowed by a great fish, engulfed in darkness and sinking fast. It reminded me of two terrifying childhood experiences.

My first experience occurred when I was six years old. My mother was a meticulous housekeeper. She made a bed with the covers pulled so tight you had to slide in from the top. As a child, I didn't feel tucked in—I felt strapped in. One night in my sleep, I apparently turned around under the covers and ended up with my head at the foot of the bed. Waking up in the middle of the night, I moved forward to get out but discovered I was completely pinned in. Frantically moving left and right in the dark, disoriented but finding no escape, I felt as if I were trapped and being buried alive. I was totally terrified. With a scream of desperation, I bolted up with all my might to throw off the covers. My current church situation felt very much the same; in the dark and disoriented, trapped and terrified; in vain I desperately tried to throw off the situation.

The second experience happened when, as a young boy at the beach, I was hit by a wave that flipped me over and under the water. With no footing, spinning round and round, I became disoriented. Seeing light above and darkness below, gasping for air and swallowing water, I felt as if I were drowning. I was desperate, enormously fearful, and panic-stricken. Fortunately, someone reached in and pulled me out. All these decades later, here I was, experiencing all those terrifying feelings afresh. But this time no one was there to pull me out.

Numb

As I slipped deeper into a dark and lonely place, I grew numb. I couldn't feel. I couldn't cry. Nothing excited me. I was shut up and shut down. I was a deeply wounded warrior, too tired to fight. I had no ability to get up, to fight, and to try it again. I had done that too often, too many times. There seemed to be nothing left to fight for, so I decided to lie down and stay down.

Depressed

I was brokenhearted over all that I had lost. Depression became my daily portion. I felt like Job sitting on an ash heap after everything he valued was taken away from him. Any enjoyment I once had in life, or any comfort I once received from anything, was gone. Looking to the future, I saw nothing but closed doors and lost hope. I despaired of any chance of change. Carefully calculating that my family would be financially taken care of if I were gone, I began to falsely believe that I was worth more dead than alive. My despair led to the wrong conclusion that everyone would be better off if I weren't here.

Deserted by God

God seemed distant, even nonexistent. All my failsafes failed. The ways I usually stayed in touch with God—my routines, my devotional time, knowledge of the Word, and even my favorite scriptures and worship songs—were all lifeless. I knew I was in trouble when the only pastime I had truly enjoyed, spending time with my grandchildren, suddenly brought me no joy. An overwhelming sense of *abandonment and loss* consumed me. It seemed like a tsunami had hit and destroyed everything and, as it receded into the sea, carried with it all I had ever loved.

Alone

The separation I had created in my approach to ministry and life now became isolation. I felt very alone. It was as if I were in solitary confinement where I couldn't get out and no visitors were allowed in. Disconnected from everyone and everything, I sat alone in the dark.

Betrayal Turned Inward

The betrayal of those closest to me was extremely painful, but now I found my own emotions betraying me. Anger at others and the circumstances turned into anger against myself. My mind betrayed me. Accusations against myself pummeled me as they screamed at me over and over again in my mind. I felt victimized by my own shortcomings. A mocking voice would shout, *What a fool you've been to give so much to gain nothing.* I concluded that maybe my father was right, I had shot marbles with my life. Replaying hundreds of scenarios from the past tormented me. At one point, I thought I was losing my mind.

Failure

I felt stripped of my identity and value. From the circumstances, I could only conclude that all my past endeavors were a failure. Worthless. My ministry of twenty-five years had been a waste of time. Like Don Quixote, I had been a romantic, making futile attempts to dream the impossible dream and fight the unbeatable foe. I concluded that I had failed not only in what I did or didn't do, but in who I was. I had failed as a pastor to God's people, failed to successfully do what God called me to do, and failed my wife, my family, and my friends. Since my identity and value were defined by success in what I did, I now redefined myself as a worthless failure.

Court-martialed

Being suddenly removed from all ministry activities, I felt as if I had been fired, laid off, and put out to pasture. Being in the military, I related it to being court-martialed—stripped of all rank and privileges, service medals removed, and my record stamped "dishonorably discharged." I concluded I was disqualified from any future ministry.

No Sure Foundation

As the bottom slid out from beneath me, I discovered shockingly that my foundation in God and my relationship with the Lord were not enough to hold me up.

Everything I had known until then—everything I had taught, everything I had trained people to do, and everything I had preached to others around the world—was not enough to keep me from sinking past any hope of return. I didn't know God deeply enough, personally enough, really enough. I didn't understand His forgiveness enough to forgive myself, to forgive my enemies, and, even more than that, to

The experience I was in was bigger than the experience of God in me.

love them. I didn't know Him as my good, good Father. There was no reality of God's love for me. I didn't grasp that He loved me despite my failures, and I wasn't sure He would save me from the darkness I was falling into. I knew I didn't deserve to be rescued and certainly hadn't earned it. I had no expectation that He would restore my joy and give me hope again.

IT'S OVER. I QUIT!

I was convinced it was too late to recover. I was done, dead, finished, through—completely fried.

The reality of what I was going through, what I was feeling, and what I was thinking was greater than the reality of God in me.

I concluded it was time to go far away, curl up in a ball, and die. Too wounded to walk, too tired to talk, too fatigued to fight, and with nothing left to say, I gave my concession speech in my heart and declared, *They win.* Like one of those extreme wrestlers in a stranglehold, I tapped out. I quit. I gave up. I turned in my badge, my uniform, and my weapons. I resigned. In my heart, I removed the signs of Pastor and Teacher from the door. I didn't put up the proverbial Gone Fishing sign; I just put up the sign Gone. I surrendered. I did it to the Lord, even though I didn't understand what it all meant. I didn't know what would happen next. All I could do for months was sit, stare at the wall—and wait.

To Be Continued

This is not the end of "My Story." Don't stop here. That would be like consigning yourself to dumpster diving when you need a good meal. In the next chapter, I will share with you what I learned from the first part of my story: how to become fried. It is what I call: "A Recipe for Fried Christian."

> *Not everyone who says to me, "Lord, Lord," will enter the kingdom of heaven, but only he who does the will of my father who is in heaven. Many will say to me on that day, "Lord, Lord, did we not prophesy in your name, and in your name drive out demons and perform many miracles?" Then I will tell them plainly, "I never knew you. Away from me, you evil doers!" (Matt. 7:21–23)*

Why should you be beaten anymore?
   Why do you persist in rebellion?
Your whole head is injured, your whole heart afflicted.
   From the soul of your foot to the top of your head there is no soundness
   —only wounds and welts and open sores, not cleansed or bandaged or soothed with oil.

(Isa. 1:5–6)

"The thief comes only to steal and kill and destroy" (John 10:10a).

Chapter Two

A Recipe For Fried Christian— How To Become Fried

NO ONE WANTS TO BE FRIED

Nobody starts out to fulfill their dreams and visions for marriage, ministry, or business with the intent to crash and burn and end up feeling like a piece of burnt toast. So why does it happen? Why have so many of us started in the light and ended up in the dark, started with hope and zeal and found ourselves hopeless and spent? Certainly, it's not a good Father who leads His children down that path.

According to Jeremiah 29:11–13, God has a plan to prosper us and not to harm us, to give us hope and a future. Is there, then, a diabolical agenda (or plan)—I am calling it a "recipe"—concocted to rob, kill, and destroy God's good plan for our lives? I think so. Unfortunately, the enemy of our souls uses toxic ingredients from within us and outside us to contaminate God's work and burn us out along the way.

I offer these lessons in the form of a recipe that, if carefully followed, will result in being fried. It is written tongue-in-cheek, knowing that nobody really wants to become fried. However, if any of the recipe's ingredients are present or any of these processes are active in your life, you may already be heading down the path of becoming a fried Christian.

> *It is my hope that the lessons I learned from the experiences I shared in "My Story, Part I—From Freedom to Fried" takes the blinders off your eyes and exposes the deadly devices of the enemy.*

THE RECIPE

The Overall Process

A good "fried Christian" requires time for the soul to marinate in the right ingredients, lots of hard work (isn't it pretty easy to get fried?), pressure, a critical crucible of crisis where all the ingredients come together, and lots of heat.

The Process: Time and Pressure

For a Christian to become a truly fried Christian, he must be in a pressure cooker for a long period of time. It is not a fast-food or microwave process. A Christian can dry out in a matter of months, but for the best results, becoming totally fried and burned out will probably take years of processing under pressure. The enemy orchestrating the process would rather fry us slowly so that we, like the proverbial frog being boiled, are oblivious to the changes taking place in us until it is too late.

Pressure can be applied in many ways: the pressure to perform perfectly, the pressure to fulfill our own and others' expectations, and the pressure from multiple crises, just to name a few. These pressures should increase and compound over an extended period of frying time. The frying process may have intervals of relief, but these should be short-lived and produce only superficial positive changes. The frying process should then continue until the Christian enters the crucible of critical crisis, the final stage to becoming totally fried to perfection. For those who are looking to cooperate with the enemy for a quicker burnout, merely double the recipe, multiply the number of crises, turn up the heat, and increase the pressure.

> **Warning**
> *This recipe for fried Christian must be followed precisely. Disregard all directions for becoming a well-done lover of God. Any mixture of the two recipes will produce a half-baked Christian.*

Very Important Note

All ingredients must be:

RAW: The ingredients of corrupt thoughts, selfish motives, and evil intents of the heart must not be purified by the Holy Spirit.

UNFILTERED: All plans, actions, works, programs, dreams, and visions should never be filtered through the Word of God.

UNPROCESSED: Ingredients such as hurts, wounds, unforgiveness, sins, thoughts, and emotions must remain unprocessed, meaning they must stay in their raw state and not undergo repentance, healing, and forgiveness.

STORED IN THE DARK: All ingredients must then be stored, warehoused, or buried in the soul. They must remain in the dark (the light of truth destroys the ingredients' potency) until they reemerge at the worst possible time to be mixed with other deadly ingredients in the burnout process.

> *For the best fried Christian, all ingredients used must be raw, unfiltered, unprocessed, and stored in the dark.*

THE SEVEN DEADLY INGREDIENTS

Ingredient 1: A Tender or a Tough Christian

The first ingredient can be one of two different types of Christian. First is the new Christian, just purchased from the butcher (the devil), very tender and trusting, full of big dreams and visions but untrained in the ways of God, His Word, and kingdom principles. The young Christian should be ignorant of the devil's devices and inexperienced in spiritual warfare. Second is an older Christian, who is never too tough to enter the process. He should have developed a strong sense of self-reliance, feeling secure in his own accomplishments and possessing perceived maturity. Although he has been around the block, he has learned little from others who burned out and has been deceived into thinking that he could never be fried.

The process is enhanced if either of these Christians has been precooked and carries wounds from their childhood, interpersonal relationships, or the church. It is helpful if they have closely adhered to indoctrinated religious principles. In either case, the Christian should have a great desire to serve the Lord and be doing the best they can. Their personal love relationship with the Lord should be shallow, and their Christian walk should center primarily on responsibilities and work. Having no mentors helps accelerate frying time and is helpful in keeping those being cooked from becoming well-done lovers of God. In addition, they should be totally ignorant of the recipe for fried Christian, its processes, and its ingredients—a perfect setup to be blindsided by the results.

Ingredient 2: The Batter

Being battered is an essential ingredient to becoming a thoroughly fried Christian. To be battered is to be struck repeatedly with heavy, violent blows; to be damaged by heavy wear; to be injured. The heavier the battering, the more it smothers the Christian, increasing the chances for becoming fried.

A good batter consists of betrayals, verbal and sexual abuses, abandonments, rejections, and lies spoken from numerous sources.

All of these add to the thickness of the batter and originate from an array of dysfunctional relationships in a person's life. Over the years, these experiences build up, creating layers of hurt and pain. It is recommended that the Christian take pride in being a wounded warrior—battered but still battling.

Self-pity is a wonderful spice to add to the battered Christian. The Christian should be in survival mode, no longer expecting to experience joy or fulfillment in anything they do. Under no circumstances should the Christian stop to be healed. Rather, they should continue to live under the battering, press past the pain, make the best of it, and work harder to change it. This will further damage the battered Christian, totally wearing them out.

> *Under no circumstances, should the Christian hinder this progression by encouraging himself in the Lord.*

It is said that wounded people wound people. Therefore, it is important for the Christian to dismiss the fact that they are wounded or that they may be wounding people in the same way they have been wounded. If the Christian wants to continue in the process toward burnout, they must chalk up hurting people to collateral damage. At this point, tender Christians become tough. They resist sensitivity to other people's pain. They are convinced that things happen and it's not their fault. Tough Christians blame problems on someone else, rationalizing that it is the cost of just trying to survive while desperately attempting to meet life's demands. Both tough and tender Christians, when well battered, are perfect candidates for the frying process.

Ingredient 3: A Full Cup of Crushed Spirit

This is a compost made from vision that became division, dreams that became nightmares, zeal that became drudgery, and hope deferred that made the heart sick. This ingredient is made by applying heavy discouragement to pulverized courage, leaving the Christian with a crushed and wounded spirit, unable to cope. The key to this ingredient is that the Christian must do the following:

- Resolve to keep on keeping on, resigned to going through the motions without emotions.

- Ignore the fact that there is no joy in what they are doing. This ingredient leaves the inner life of the Christian filled with quiet desperation, screaming and crying on the inside while smiling and pretending on the outside.

- Never stop to refuel when the empty light flashes; instead, run on fumes until completely out of gas. When the engine light comes on, they should ignore it and not pull into a shop for repairs.

- Pay no attention to a loss of faith and hope. Keep working hard.

- Be convinced that the light at the end of the tunnel is not an oncoming train.

- Continue down the road of the "four Ds": from disappointment, to discouragement, into depression, and finally into despair.

Ingredient 4: A Pound of Principles from the Pit

It is important in the frying of a Christian that the ungodly and humanistic principles used by the devil to bring about burnout remain hidden. By remaining as a stronghold in the soul, these demonic principles can continue to operate in the life of the Christian and bring destruction.

I like to think of these principles as driving forces—the core values, assumptions, and personal worldviews we live by. At times, we are not even aware of the unconscious thought patterns that frame the way we do life or the subliminal rules that drive our behavior. Based on our experiences, environment, and education, we also form prejudices in the way we relate to ourselves, others, and the world around us. It wasn't until I, under the direction of the Holy Spirit, really peeled back the layers and uncovered these principles—that is, named and identified them—that I started the process of moving from fried to well-done.

While my list is long and extensive, each of these principles from the pit played its part in my frying process. See if you can identify with any of these operating in your life:

- It's a battle, so never surrender. This is an ungodly principle that unfortunately works against you in your relationship with the Lord.
- It's not how many times you fall or fail, but how many times you get up. (But what if you can't get up?)

- If it doesn't work, work harder. Burning out is better than rusting out.
- There is no vacation from vocation.
- You're only as good as your last good deed, sale, or sermon.
- Succumb to the tyranny of the urgent. Given all the "important" things you have to do, rest and recreation feel like a waste of time.
- Be who you are. Some worship because they are worshipers. Some pray because they are prayer warriors. But me? I'm a worker, not a worshiper; I pray on the way.
- Read the Word to get a quick word for the day or a fresh message to preach or teach to others, but not to simply sit, meditate, and wait upon the Lord.

> *When necessary, do God-things without God.*

- Stay strong. Never be vulnerable and admit your weaknesses. People will take advantage of you, disrespect you, and stop listening to you.
- Measure success against others' accomplishments (marriage, career, ministry). Resist the fact that comparisons make you feel inadequate.
- Don't admit that you're competitive or jealous; call it striving for excellence.
- Don't celebrate either small or large achievements. There's always more to do.
- Stay in abusive relationships or situations, rationalizing that God will make you stronger through it.

A Recipe for Fried Christian

- Expect perfection from yourself and others.
- Learn to play hurt, and don't come off the field when injured.
- If God is distant or not moving in a situation, do without God the thing He gave you to do, and call it faithful obedience.
- Operate on presumption, not personal revelation. If it's in His Word, obey it and expect God to bless it.
- Hold on to relationships, plans, and programs that are fruitless and unproductive.
- Set goals for yourself and others that are impossible to reach.
- Remind yourself that God rewards those who work hard and earn it.
- Believe that people don't tell you the truth and are not honest most of the time.
- Live out of your head, not your heart.
- Strive to be everything to all people all the time.
- No one does it better than you. So micromanage, control, and redo what you've entrusted to others.
- Ignore and excuse your small character flaws, attitude problems, and besetting sins. Forget that,

> *If you want to continue frying, under no circumstances should you invite the Holy Spirit to search and uncover the principles from the pit that are operating in your life.*

according to Wikipedia, it was a small, inexpensive gasket leaking fuel that caused the *Challenger* to explode in 1986, killing seven astronauts, costing $3.2 billion, and delaying the advancement of the space program for over two years.

Ingredient 5: A Container of Corrupted Common Sense

Common sense is corrupted when we make foolish judgments, refuse sound counsel, and act and speak rashly out of a place of ignorance or pride. A full container of this is essential to the recipe for creating a fried Christian.

Here are some further insights into how corrupted common sense played an integral part in my personal recipe for becoming fried:

- Don't ask for help or take wise counsel to heart. Other people, no matter how experienced or professional, don't totally understand you or your situation.

- Violate your intuition. Avoid listening to the deep knowing in your spirit, since it will require courage and honesty to stand firm in the face of opposing opinions.

- Succumb to the fear of man, and follow the path of peace at any price.

- Ignore red flags. These warnings, if valid, will threaten your dreams and visions and only slow you down in reaching your goals. Run stop signs, don't yield at yellow lights, and blow through all the red ones.

- Continue to herd cats, spin plates, and build sand castles on an incoming tide. Despite the frustration of seeing things fall apart around you, continue to give your all to make it work. When the cats won't listen, put them on leashes or get other cats. When a plate crashes to the ground, get another plate and keep spinning. When a breaking wave wipes out the castle, build another one in the exact same spot with higher and thicker walls. Practice the definition of insanity: doing the same thing and expecting different results.

- Learn to live in quiet desperation as you attempt to make new wine out of a handful of grapes (a new marriage, a new career, a new ministry).

- Continue to bury and warehouse your feelings. Do not share them with someone you trust. Your obsession with how people perceive you—fearing they will see you as weak and misunderstood—speeds up the frying time.

- Time is a nonrenewable asset. Use it to work hard 24/7. If you're not physically working, make sure to work by worrying. And think, think, think. This helps greatly in burning out your brain.

- Don't pray or wait on God for His direction, counsel, instruction, and timing.

- Compromise your calling and gifts to please others. Believe that if you don't please them, they will leave you (marriage, career, or ministry).

- Let the sun go down on your anger. Let unforgiveness and offense build up in your gut until it turns to bitterness. Marinate your soul in bitterness by constantly dwelling on others' offenses against you.

- Be in love with the goal more than with the people. Lead people by motivating them to accomplish the end goal. If they do not get on board, push and drive them instead of loving and encouraging them.

- Prioritize family, career, and ministry before time with the Lord and your spouse. Be married to your career or ministry before being married to your spouse.

- Put the Great Commission before both the Great Commandment and the Golden Rule.

- Be a different person to fit different situations, like a chameleon that changes its colors to suit its environment.

- Make no time for rest and recreation. Do not play, take a walk on the beach, stare at the stars at night, or just veg. If you take a break as a concession to your family or from a strong directive from your friends or co-laborers, take work with you. Do not take deep breaths.

Be purpose-driven, not love-motivated.

- Neglect personal health and wellness, including regular physical exercise and a nutritious diet. Rely on high amounts of caffeine and sugar to keep you going.

- Take yourself too seriously. Don't laugh at yourself.

- Talk at people, not with people.

Ingredient 6: Ten Pints of Prideful Persistence

Prideful persistence is an active ingredient that causes all the other ingredients to coagulate. While each principle from the pit plays its role in frying the Christian, when prideful persistence is added to the mix, it increases the potency of all the other ingredients in the recipe. Prideful persistence finds its identity and worth in a performance-based mentality: you are what you do. It almost always resists admitting faults, failures, and weaknesses. The pridefully persistent Christian adopts a "my way or the highway" type of thinking and is quick to correct or redo anything not done the way they want it. Sadly, since one of their greatest fears is losing control, they become defensive, dig in, and push back even in the face of constructive criticism, especially when feeling threatened. Finally, the pridefully persistent person seeks to be first—thanked, honored, and appreciated for everything they do. When efforts go unnoticed, they become angry or even depressed.

This candidate for burnout begins to fulfill the definition of insanity stated earlier: doing the same thing and expecting different results. This person engages in a never-ending stream of negative self-talk that keeps him pridefully persistent. Here are some of the thoughts and premises that drove my life from the backseat: Never surrender. Press on, as this could be the time for victory. Even a broken clock is right twice a day. Disregard the advice of the pros. (A golf instructor once told me that getting new equipment would never change my swing, and that continuing to play without

Warning: Any change of heart may not only dilute or delay the process to burnout, but may completely destroy it.

changing the fundamentals would never improve my game.)

Sincerity is not a factor here. You can be sincere in what you're doing and be sincerely wrong. You can hide behind thinking you are a good person yet not live in the truth. The same goes for good intentions. It is said that the road to hell is paved with good intentions. You can be well-intentioned but on the wrong road and thus will never get to where you want to go.

If you want to be a thoroughly fried Christian, change the externals only. Never cave to the need to change anything fundamental about yourself from the inside out. Whether it's your marriage, ministry, or career, keep packing on different approaches that promise to fix the problem without doing the heart work necessary for true transformation. Keep putting Band-Aids on a cancer. Go to the gurus of the world for a quick fix. Try every "Ten Steps to Success in Ten Days" program that you can find, showing you how to fix your marriage, how to be successful in business, or how to grow your church. And when these don't work, try another program. Convince yourself that due to the lack of time and the pressure to perform, you need a quick fix for a deep, long-term problem.

So, stay committed to becoming fried and whatever you do, do not surrender to the Lord. Do not wait upon Him for an answer from heaven. Do not repent and turn.

Ingredient 7: A Large Ladle of Lethal Lies

Jesus said that our enemy, the devil, has been a liar from the beginning. This enemy advances his process of frying a Christian by getting the Christian to believe subtle and destructive lies. The Christian believes they are living in the truth, but in reality, they are deceived and actually living in lies. If you are to stay in the frying process you must never judge what you believe against the truth of God's Word.

Here are some of the key lies that lead to being fried:

- **Lies about love**—One of the most lethal lies Christians believe is that they are loved for what they do, not for who they are. They may also come to believe that they are loved only for what others can get from them. Conversely, frying victims continue to seek to fill their love vacuums with the conditional love of other people, leaving them mostly empty and frustrated. Believing lies about love drives them to hunger for the recognition, acceptance, and affirmation of others, in stark contrast to the security found in knowing they are unconditionally loved by God. Christians in the process of being fried base their love for God and God's love for them on their own ability and merit in getting everything perfect and obeying His commands.

- **Lies about father relationships**—Christians in the frying process often live as though God the Father is just like their fathers on earth. This deep, hidden, subliminal lie deceives them into believing that the way their earthly fathers loved them is the way God loves them. Without being consciously aware of it, these Christians live as if their earthly fathers' absence, silence, abuse, and neglect mirror the way God treats them. They are burdened by a nagging need to be perfect as a prerequisite to earning the Father's love, affirmation, and approval.

- **Lies about failure**—To a deceived Christian undergoing the frying process, failure is the concrete evidence that they are "not enough": not qualified enough, gifted enough, blessed enough, strong enough, or didn't work hard enough. The verdict that renders them "not as good as" deceives them into thinking that only the chosen few around them are succeeding. They secretly believe in their heart that God doesn't really love them or desire to bless them and see them succeed. They come to believe that they are being punished for not being perfect. *A Christian with failure issues has bought the lie that God has favorites, and that they are not one of them.* They are trapped in a failure cycle. Failure is an invitation to quit, but quitting is failure, so they keep trying until they fail again. In all their efforts, they will succeed at one thing: becoming fried.

- **Lies about abandonment**—A Christian in the frying process succumbs to the lie that they need someone on earth to love them, approve them, affirm them, secure them, and give them identity. They will pursue specific people to fulfill these basic needs in them. When these people fail to meet their needs—leaving them disappointed, angry, and empty—they switch their pursuit to others. When everyone inevitably fails them, they feel abandoned and conclude they are unwanted, unloved, unacceptable, and without value. This deceived and wounded Christian may develop a defense against these unmet needs by determining that they don't need anyone. By doing this, they then avoid and guard themselves against entering meaningful relationships, attempting to protect themselves from ever being hurt again. Now, wounded and isolated, they indulge in worldly novocaine to deaden the pain. They work hard to fill the void with activity and material things on the outside while remaining desperately empty on the inside.

- **Lies about identity**—Having accepted the four lies above, this Christian is on the fast track to being fried. They will take on the identity of an orphan—fatherless, rejected, having low self-esteem, feeling unloved, unacceptable, unworthy, worthless, and unaccomplished in their own estimation. Though there may be a few positive relationships in their life, they are nevertheless convinced that nobody loves them. Taking on the orphan identity, they wallow in secret shame fully expecting to be continuously rejected.

In summary, with these lies in operation, the Christian actually begins to live out of a false identity whose framework is built around what they do, what they have accomplished, or what they possesses. They take pride in their own self-sufficiency and believe they can live life independently of other people, reconciling themselves to the fact that the only time they feel worth anything, loved or accepted, is when they have worked for something and accomplished it. As a result, they work hard, pouring themselves into becoming a self-made person. Finally, living out of this ladle of lies causes the Christian to fry in various degrees of self-pity, condemnation, shame, anger, isolation, and obnoxious pride.

CONFLICT IN THE KITCHEN

It is recommended that the Christian on the path to being fried spend a great amount of time in an environment that promotes the frying process. It has been said that too many cooks spoil the broth. Similarly, Christians in marriage, ministry, or business relationships where conflicting visions, multiple philosophies, and differing core values and theologies are present are prone to frying faster than others. That's because *two visions are di-vision.* A house divided against itself not only cannot stand, but also threatens to keep those involved from ever becoming well-done. The stress on the Christian from continuous chaos and constant conflict in primary relationships accelerates the frying process. Therefore, beware of agreement, teamwork, unity, honoring one another, and submission to God-ordained headship. These are enemies of chaos and will dismantle conflict, thus thwarting the frying process.

THE CRUCIBLE OF CRITICAL CRISIS

This is the final stage in becoming a fried Christian. Up until now, the besieged Christian has managed to keep their head above water in their own strength. However, like quick sand, over a long period of time, they have slowly, almost imperceptibly, sunk until they are now pulled under and can no longer breathe. This is when the mother of all crises hits. It's the straw that breaks the camel's back. It's their Waterloo. It's a perfect storm of all the carefully prepared ingredients colliding together. All their "enemies" have congealed, consorting together to hit them with the full force of a tsunami.

Despite the fact that the Christian has had many warnings of this approaching storm and has had a long time to prepare for it and numerous opportunities to divert it, it still catches them off guard. It feels like a devastating surprise attack—like Pearl Harbor or 9/11. They are spinning in shock. It's surreal but too real at the same time. The heat is turned up to the max. They feel trapped, surrounded, pushed into a corner with nowhere to run, hide, or escape. They are alone, gripped with fear, out of strength, out of answers, and out of control. The bottom has fallen out of everything they have always relied on to hold them up. They now free fall into darkness. Wounded, down, and defenseless, the battered Christian waits for the demonic process to move in for the final kill. It's over—they are finished, cooked, burned out, fried.

DON'T DESPAIR

I pray this horrendous experience never happens to you. However, if you recognize the ingredients of this recipe operating in your life and have continued in the process to completion, regretfully, you've made it. You are a bona-fide, full-fledged, totally fried Christian.

Don't despair, my friend. Your Redeemer lives! In the next chapter, I will share the second part of my story: how the Lord brought me from fried to well-done and how He is re-creating me into a well-done lover of God. He did it for me, and He will do it for you!

Part Two

How to Become a Well-Done Lover of God

He was despised and rejected by men,
  a man of sorrows, and familiar with suffering.
Like one from whom men hide their faces
  he was despised, and we esteemed him not.
Surely he took up our infirmities and carried our sorrows,
  yet we considered him stricken by God,
  smitten by him, and afflicted.
But he was pierced for our transgressions,
  he was crushed for our iniquities;
the punishment that brought us peace was upon him,
  and by his wounds we are healed. (Isa. 53:3–5)

The spirit of the sovereign Lord is on me,
  because the Lord has anointed me to preach good news to the poor.
He has sent me to bind up the brokenhearted, to
  proclaim freedom for the captives and
  release from darkness for the prisoners,
to proclaim the year of the Lord's favor
  and the day of vengeance of our God,
to comfort all who mourn, and provide for those
  who grieve in Zion–
to bestow on them a crown of beauty instead of ashes,
  the oil of gladness instead of mourning,
  and a garment of praise instead of a spirit of despair.
They will be called oaks of righteousness, a planting
  of the Lord for the display of his splendor. (Isa. 61:1-3)

"But the father said to his servants, 'Quick! Bring the best robe and put it on him. Put a ring on his finger and sandals on his feet. Bring the fatted calf and kill it. Let's have a feast and celebrate. For this son of mine was dead and is alive again; he was lost and is found. So they began to celebrate." (Luke 15:22–24)

"I have come that they may have life, and have it to the full." (Jn.10:10b)

Chapter Three

My Story, Part II— From Fried to Well-Done

WHAT HAPPENED NEXT

Let me pick up where I left off in "My Story, Part I— From Freedom to Fried." I had quit and surrendered to the Lord and was totally numb for months. What happened next can only be credited to God and God alone. His faithfulness, His love, His grace, His mercy, and His forgiveness reached down and touched me. He was true to His promise that He would never leave me nor forsake me. Suddenly His light broke through the darkness. I felt Him catch me in my free fall. His Spirit swept beneath me and lifted me up.

He Wrapped Me

I intuitively knew He had accepted my resignation and had been waiting for me to completely surrender to Him. I then heard Him say in my heart, *"What took you *so long?"* At that moment, it was as if He wrapped me in a baby bunting, causing me to feel secure and safe. He gathered me like a little lamb with broken legs, put me on His shoulders, and carried me. I sensed He was there. He was with me, holding me, and deep down inside, I knew everything was going to be okay.

The Honeymoon

For the next six months, He took me away to a solitary place, isolating me from all activity and keeping me alone with Him. As if I were in a cocoon, He began transforming me from the inside out—instructing me, correcting me, adjusting me, changing my heart and mind, healing my wounded soul, and teaching me His ways. It was a spiritual honeymoon that I hadn't experienced since I was first saved. I felt loved, in love, and carefree. He was drawing out of me a love for Him that had never been there, in a way I had never experienced—a full-faced, first-love relationship with Jesus.

> *During this time, He restrained me from asking questions or even needing answers.*

Never once was there an ounce of condemnation from Him. He never brought up my shortcomings, faults, failures, or sins.

How Great Thou Art

At the beginning, during our daily "walk and talk" times, I was silent as He spoke volumes, revealing Himself in nature all around me. In the morning, the sun seemed brighter, the grass was greener, the birds were singing songs I had never heard, and my little dog's wiggle when she walked amused me. At night, the stars were a magnificent display of beauty in the darkness, the moon and it's phases a dramatic lesson in transition. In all of this, God was showing Himself to me as majestic, awesome, holy, and beautiful. He revealed Himself as loving in all He did.

He became a source of perfect wonder to me. From deep within me, praise began to burst forth for all He was showing me. Everything He created was so "well done." I felt as if a great stone that had been placed on my deepest well was being removed; the cork was coming out of the bottle of my heart, and I began effervescing with joyful sounds. I was singing songs I had never heard before.

He also put the classic worship song, "How Great Thou Art," on my heart. I had to look up the words because I had never learned them. I would sing it on our walks together as He displayed His magnificent creation, and it has now become my favorite worship song:

> *Oh, Lord my God, when I in awesome wonder,*
> *Consider all the worlds Thy hands have made.*
> *I see the stars, I hear the rolling thunder,*
> *Thy power throughout the universe displayed.*
> *Then sings my soul, my Savior God to Thee,*
> *How great Thou art, how great Thou art.*

Thanksgiving followed the chorus of praise. I would thank Him and thank Him again for everything that I had ever experienced, everything I was experiencing, and everything about Himself that He was revealing to me.

Little by little, day by day, He led me out of a dry desert place into an ocean of His love. The display of His beauty in creation resulted in heartfelt praise, thanksgiving, and singing, which in turn created a symphony whose melody and message from God to me was: *I love you more than all of My creation. I love you with an everlasting love. I created you for Myself to be loved by Me, and for you to love Me with all your being. You are My son and I am your Father.*

He did it! He saved me. With loving kindness he tore through the shadows of my soul, burst into the prison of my pain, and lifted me up into a vibrant love relationship with Him. I was born again, again. It was a brand new beginning. All praise to the name of Jesus!

NEW ROOTS

Converted to Living Inside Out

After a few months of honeymooning with the Lord, I felt an urge rising up inside me to get going, to get back on my horse and ride, to start doing something. If nothing else, I wanted to go tell people what was happening to me. The Lord, however, caused me to wait upon Him. When I thought I was finished waiting, He instructed me to wait some more. He told me to wait, and then wait, and then wait some more, until I was renewed and He was ready to release me. I was far too quick to want to get up and go back to old ways, old thinking, old patterns, and old reliance on myself rather than Him. Fortunately, He would not allow me to jump off His shoulders and go skipping off. I still knew too little of who He was.

The Lord had more to reveal to me, more to make real to me. I still needed to soak in His presence and be saturated in His love until it re-formed me into His image as a son. In this process, He was reorienting me and converting me from living primarily from the "outside in"—based on my thoughts, emotions, needs, outside influences, and what I thought He should be doing or what I should be doing for Him—to living from the "inside out" by the Spirit. Through this rewiring, I was learning to live in an intimate relationship, knowing Him and His amazing love experientially. *He rooted out my old identity as a self-centered servant and planted me in my new identity as a Christ-centered son.* He was shifting my control center from my head to my heart.

I came to know I was loved, not for what I did, but for who I was. He was transforming me from a worker into a worshiper.

Dismantled Errant Principles

The Lord dismantled errant principles that I had long lived by. I remember the first one He dealt with. In a quiet time, He gently and simply asked me, *Dennis, when I called you into the ministry, what was it that I called you to?*

I answered, "Oh Lord, that's easy. Matthew 28:18 has always been my life scripture, my marching orders: '…go and make disciples of all nations,' I've done that. I've gone to as many nations as You've opened to me. I preached the gospel and became fried doing it."

Then He asked me one simple question: *Dennis, when did the Great Commission supersede the Great Commandment?* Of course, when the Lord asks a question, there really isn't any answer. It's rhetorical.

"Love the Lord, your God, with your whole heart, mind, soul, and strength," I responded. "You know, Lord, that I love You, and I've shown my love to You by being obedient."

He replied, *No, that's not what you are to do first. Before you are a worker, you are to be a worshiper—to love Me, to be loved by Me, to spend time with Me. It's not about time in the field; it's about time in My presence.*

The One Thing

I admitted to the Lord that I really didn't know enough about who He is. I admitted that, unfortunately, what I did know had not been enough to keep me from becoming fried. But I told Him I wanted to know Him more, to see Him for who He truly is. It became obvious to me that much of the information I had about Him was not a revelational experience of Him. *I had much head knowledge, but I needed more heart (spirit) knowledge.* I asked Him, therefore, to give me a full-faced love relationship with Jesus.

This plea began the next phase of my spiritual walk with the Lord. The Holy Spirit began to deepen my understanding by revelation of the moral attributes of God: His love, His faithfulness, His righteousness, and His holiness. I came to realize that through Christ Jesus, I am the righteousness of God (2 Cor. 5:21), made in His image and likeness. These revelations gave me a firmer sense of

His presence *with* me and *in* me (Jn.14:17b). The reality of the presence of Jesus has become my "one thing"—and the only thing—I want more of every day of my life.

Revelations of who He is in me and who I am in Him have convinced me that the Father loves me and that I am His beloved son. I know now that He has forgiven me, washed me, healed me, and is actively forming me into the image of His Son, Jesus. I have not earned it, nor will I ever be able to thank Him enough for His freely given lavish love.

Joy

In those first months of personal revival, I experienced a joy I had never known before. It was a joy based, not on what happens, who I am, or what I do, but based on who He is, what He has done, and His extravagant, enduring love for me. My joy level is now my barometer to determine just how much I am experiencing God living inside me and how much I am living out of being in His presence, beholding His majesty, beauty, holiness, glory, and power. My joy level also indicates how much I am living in the fullness of expressing my love to Him. Thanksgiving and praise are the fire starters of joy and the means by which I enter into His presence. As I wait in His presence, I come to know by the Spirit the fullness of His love for me, and I return my love for Him in worship. There in His presence, I experience the fullness of His joy—joy unspeakable and filled with glory.

Rest

Deep rest came to my soul as I trusted Jesus more. I was no longer working, striving, fighting, or trying to gain approval, acceptance, status, or possessions. The work was done—He did it. It was finished, and I could rest in that. He loved me. The fear of failure had vanished. I had never felt more secure in all my life. I totally trusted that He would lead me forth from where I had been to where He wanted me to go. I knew that I would become what He wanted me to be. Why? Because He is working, and I am resting in His working.

> *He is working, and I am resting in His working.*

The pressure of responsibility was lifted from me. In fact, my definition of responsibility changed to "my response but His ability."

Transformation

I have come to realize that His goal is to transform me into His very image and likeness. Then, by His grace, out of who I am will come what I do for His glory.

> *The Lord will speak the words "well done" over my life, not for what I've done, but for who I have become—"good and faithful."*

THE CHALLENGES

Love your enemies

Shortly after my personal revival, the Lord presented me with a challenge. He asked me if I loved my enemies. I told him that I had forgiven everyone, but I knew in my heart that I did not have love for certain ones. At a conference I had planned to go to there was a possibility of meeting those that I had forgiven but didn't have love for. I knew if I went and bumped into them, it was going to be very uncomfortable. I wasn't ready to see them, so I decided not to go.

Nevertheless, the night before the conference, I wrestled for hours with the Lord about this. He showed me Matthew 5:44: "But I tell you: love your enemies and pray for those who persecute you, that you may be sons of your Father in heaven." That scared me. I didn't want anything to jeopardize my relationship with the Lord. I confessed that if I were to love them, He would have to put that love in my heart. Miraculously at 1 o'clock in the morning, He did it! He gave me love for them.

I went to the conference the next day, and sure enough, they were there. But amazingly, I felt overwhelming love for them. I went to each of them, hugged them, kissed them, and told each one that I loved them. Taken by surprise, they were speechless. But the victory was won—the Lord had healed the wound in my heart. Subsequently, most of these relationships have been restored. Spiritual sons and daughters I had lost have been returned. Through this experience, the Lord moved me to another level of becoming well-done.

The Ongoing Battles

Since then, the continuing process to becoming well-done has not been easy. There have been many battles, many highs, and many lows.

In the beginning of this new adventure with the Lord, the smallest failure, shortcoming, weakness, or any rejection from others reminded me of my old identity and tempted me to accept it, with all the old feelings waiting to flood in. However, in every conflict, the Lord has faithfully broken through, taking me aside, reaffirming His love for me, quickening my love for Him, and refreshing the lessons He has taught me in the process. Over time, my temptations to fall back have become fewer and farther between as I've grown more grounded in my new identity. The Lord has used my weaknesses to display His strength and magnify His unconditional, faithful love for me in spite of my fragile love for Him.

The greatest attacks from the enemy of my soul are against my identity as a beloved son of God.

My lows have served only as a platform for Him to reveal Himself in new ways, pull up old roots, and deepen my love relationship with Him. Battling the tendency to revert to old patterns rooted in a performance-based mentality have strengthened my resolve to come aside, be still, stay surrendered, wait upon the Lord, and walk and talk with Him. Spending quality face-to-face time in His presence is my safe harbor, my happy place, and my greatest joy. Thanksgiving, praise, and worship have become not just powerful weapons I use against the enemy of my soul, and an effective strategy against my regressive tendencies, but a way of life to continually experience the blessing of God's presence anytime, anywhere.

MY STORY IS NOT OVER

The Continuing Process

Very far from being fried, I am nevertheless not finished. I continue in the process to becoming well-done, transformed more and more into Jesus's image. I have been changed, and I am being changed. I have been re-formed, and I am being re-formed. I have been renewed, and I am being renewed.

Confident and Convinced

I know the Lord will accomplish everything He has planned for me, and it will be well-done. Continually returning to resting and trusting Him has become my default setting. When He deems I am finished processing here on earth and it is time to meet Him face-to-face, I am confident I will hear those words from the lover of my soul, my Savior and Lord, Jesus Christ: "Well done, good and faithful servant. You have been faithful in a little, now enter into the joy of your Master."

He has worked and will continue to work until I am well-done. He is faithful. He is good. He is love. He alone will receive all the praise and all the glory.

In the next chapter, I will share the lessons I learned that taught me: how to become a well-done lover of God.

Therefore, I urge you, brothers, in view of God's mercy, to offer your bodies as living sacrifices, holy and pleasing to God—this is your spiritual act of worship. Do not conform any longer to the pattern of this world, but be transformed by the renewing of your mind. Then you will be able to test and approve what God's will is—his good, pleasing and perfect will.
(Rom. 12:1–2)

My lover spoke and said to me,
"Arise, my darling, my beautiful one, and come with me."
Place me like a seal over your heart, like a seal on your arm;
for love is as strong as death, it's jealousy unyielding as the grave.
It burns like blazing fire, like a mighty flame.
Many waters cannot quench love; rivers cannot wash it away.
(S of S. 2:10; 8:6-7)

Dear friends, let us love one another, for love comes from God. And so we know and rely on the love God has for us. God is love. Whoever lives in love lives in God, and God in him.
(1 Jn.4:7a,16)

Chapter Four

How to Become a Well-Done Lover of God

EVERYBODY WANTS TO FINISH WELL

I believe everyone on life's journey—in marriage, ministry, or career—wants to finish well. We all want to hear someone say, "Well done." Having started out with that noble ambition, I nevertheless ended up fried. In "My Story, Part II," I shared my experiences of how the Lord turned my ashes into beauty and gave me the oil of gladness for mourning and a garment of praise for a spirit of despair. Those experiences put me on a path of becoming what I call a "well-done lover of God." Matthew 25:21 tells us that Jesus acknowledges good and faithful servants with the words *well done*. While it is a play on words, nevertheless, the Lord desires for us to become well-done, not fried. Just as in the burning bush that Moses experienced, the Lord wants us on fire but not burned out.

The following is a summary of the lessons I learned from these experiences. It is my hope that they will guide you to progress toward your own "well done."

THE PURPOSES, PROCESSES, AND PLACES FOR BECOMING WELL DONE

Being aligned with God's purposes is essential to ending up well-done. If we don't know where we're going, we probably won't get there. If we know where the finish line is, however, it will help us chart the course to win the race and gain the prize.

In "My Story, Part I," I shared that I was very much out of alignment with God's primary purposes. Driven to perform, I believed doing things for the Lord in obedience to His commands would gain me a "well done." I shared with you all the pain that produced. In "My Story, Part II," I shared that through these experiences, I came

> *I came to understand that it's not what you've done but who you've become that pleases the Lord the most.*

to understand that it's not what you've done but who you've become that pleases the Lord the most. He taught me that He's looking for my transformation into a "good and faithful servant," a son in the image of Jesus, more than any work that I might perform.

In Matthew 7:21–23, Jesus makes it clear that it is possible to find ourselves in the unfortunate position of saying, "Lord, Lord, did we not prophesy in your name, and in your name drive out demons, and perform many miracles?" and for Him to respond, "I never knew you. Away from me, you evildoers (workers of iniquity, workers of self-will)." I realize now that we can labor without love or obey the letter of the Word by doing good works without having an intimate relationship with the Lord or His love in our hearts. *I've learned it is possible to do God-things without God.* It's possible to do the works of Christ without being like Christ in our character.

In one of His first fundamental corrections, He showed me that ultimately He is not looking for good works, but rather, our conformity to Christ. This is the major alignment: to be transformed into the very image and likeness of Jesus. Romans 8:29 tells us that those God always knew He predestined to be conformed to the likeness of His Son. Second Corinthians 3:18 says that we, with an unveiled face-to-face relationship, while reflecting the Lord's glory, are being transformed into His likeness.

Love: The Key Ingredient

Being transformed into the image and likeness of Jesus necessitates that we become one with Him in His nature of love. First John 4:16 says, "God is love. Whoever lives in love lives in God, and God in him." Jesus expands the purpose for us to be in a love union with Him in John 17:23, "I (Jesus) in them and you (Father) in me. May they be brought to complete unity *to let the world know* that you sent me and have loved them even as you have loved me."(emphasis added)

In summary, to become well-done lovers of God, we must become aligned with the multiple purposes of God: to be transformed into the image of Jesus, to be merged into a love union with Jesus and the Father, and to become a tangible expression of the Father's love so that the world will believe in Jesus.

THE PROCESSES FOR BECOMING WELL-DONE

These are the processes I have discovered the Father uses (present tense, ongoing) to transform us into a well-done son or daughter conformed to the image of Christ. It has become apparent to me that the Father is more concerned with our conformity to Christ than with our comfort. Because He loves us, He will allow any amount of discomfort to bring about His perfect will for our lives so that we are transformed into a perfect image of His Son. He loves us so much that He will allow to come into our lives circumstances and people that the enemy has meant for evil and use them to destroy what is keeping us from having an intimate relationship with Him and fulfilling our destinies.

In Genesis 50:20, we see that Joseph went through years of processing that began with his brothers' betrayal and ended with his becoming the second in command to Pharaoh. At the end of his processes, he was able to say to his brothers, "You intended to harm me, but God intended it for good to accomplish what is now being done, the saving of many lives." God has a plan for those He loves and causes all things to work together for their good and His glory (Rom. 8:28).

As we see in Joseph's life, the Lord will use these processes in a multitude of ways: (1) to expose sin, attitudes, motives of the heart, lies we have believed, humanistic thinking, worldly principles, idols and religious practices;

(2) to heal us of wounds through love and forgiveness; (3) to train us in the ways of His kingdom; (4) to transform us from the inside out into His beloved sons and daughters, and (5) to bring us into the fullness of his plans and purposes for our life. He is totally committed to removing any obstacle that is keeping us from His eternal goal of having sons and daughters who know His love, love Him with all their hearts, and will be ambassadors of His kingdom on earth as it is in heaven.

When the Lord of glory comes into our tabernacles to begin these processes and overturns the tables of our hearts, upsetting our status quo and everything that inhibits intimacy with Him, it can feel very disturbing, even violent, at times. But He is jealous for our love and determined for us to become our Father's house of prayer and worship for all nations (Jn. 2:13-16). This is a caution for anyone who wants to be well-done: Don't give place for anything to operate in your temple that He will only have to remove out of love by His power.

> *Don't give place for anything to operate in your temple that He will only have to remove out of love by His power.*

His processes will realign us with His kingdom principles. Tires that are out of alignment wear out very quickly and endanger the travelers with blowouts. The Lord will go after even the smallest inconsistencies with the character of His Son, Jesus. Why? Because the smallest things can destroy the biggest plans God has for our lives. Remember the Challenger explosion. Selah.

The Lord will use numerous processes to correct the fundamentals in the way we do life. New programs, procedures, and practices do not change our character. Encounters with God will. The processes of the Lord are continuous, they overlap, and they recycle. The order and priority of the processes are totally up to the Lord. They are all important, and He knows how to coordinate them to form us into the individually well-done lovers He designed us to be. Additionally, we can be in more than one process at the same time. The intensity and duration of any process depends on what He wants to accomplish in us and our degree of cooperation with Him. The key then is to trust Him, to be content, and to stay in the processes. *I am convinced I will never be done until I stand before him and get my "well done."*

Process 1: From Trash to Transformation

This is the overall process the Lord brings us through to produce a well-done lover of God. Other processes deal in more specific areas of our lives. Through people, pressure, and persecution, the Lord will purge and purify all of the trash stored in our souls. He has led me through times of brokenness before Him; confession of my sins, failures, shortcomings, and weaknesses; and repentance for all that was out of line with the character of Christ. In this process, I asked Him for mercy and grace. Humbled before Him, I asked for His forgiveness, then extended forgiveness to those who had offended me. When

> *The process is garbage out and goodness in.*

necessary, He directed me to go to others that I had offended to seek their forgiveness. He taught me to use my authority in Christ to gain deliverance from demonic influences that oppressed my soul.

Transformation is accomplished as He brings us through the succeeding processes.

Process 2: From Reduction to Production

To produce the image of Christ in us and make us useful to the Master, the Lord uses a process common to Joseph, Moses, David, Peter, and Paul. Each of them was stripped of his former identity, security, comforts, titles, gifts, strengths, and self-sufficiency. Each of them faced enemies, both within and without, that drove them into obscurity, separated them from everything they knew, and thrust them into a dark night of the soul. Over a period of time, even years, each of them came to the end of themselves. The Lord took all the fight, bitterness, and self-will out of them and brought them into a new revelation of who He is and who they were in Him.

> *God will prune us in order to prosper us on the road to becoming well-done.*

John 15 says that branches (us) that are producing a little fruit will be pruned so they produce much fruit.

It is a painful process that the Father, the husbandman, applies because He loves us. What God is looking to produce through the reduction process is a person surrendered and submitted to His will, someone who is obedient, humbled, crushed and re-created, poor in spirit, emptied of relying on human strength and ambition, and moving only in the power of His Spirit.

Process 3: From Information to Revelation; From Conflicted to Convinced

It is one thing to know all about the Lord, and even teach and train others what you know intellectually, but it is another thing altogether to know the Lord by personal experience and personal revelation. It is one thing to know all about love and all the Greek words that describe love, but it is extraordinarily different to know deep inside you that God is love, that He loves you, is for you, is in you, is the very source and foundation of your life and will impart this love to you to love others through you. It is revelational experiences that creates in a person a deep realization of the magnitude of Christ's incredible love in all its magnificent dimensions. This love transcends our mental ability to comprehend. Coming to know His love deep within our spirits, a love that surpasses sense knowledge (Eph. 3:17–18), revolutionizes our lives. It was one thing for me to stand at the bedside of my wife as she gave birth, but it was a totally different experience for her as she actually birthed a child. Revelational experiences supersede intellectual knowledge.

Paul declared in Romans 8:38 that nothing could separate him from God's love. Frankly, I was never totally convinced and always conflicted with the fact that God actually loved me just for who I am. I could not fully thank Him for what He had done, praise Him for what He was doing, or worship Him for who He is. I was not convinced that He was love—a good, good Father, faithful, sovereign, in control of my life and the world, and all-wise in everything He did. My life's experiences, coupled with my outside-in worldview and understandings, conflicted with who He said He was. As a result, before He began revealing His magnificent attributes to me, I was stuck in elder-son religion (Luke 15:25–32), pharisaical legalism (Saul's zeal before he became Paul), and performance-based Christianity.

> *I prayed puny prayers, offered pitiful praise, and gave only tepid thanksgiving and wimpy worship.*

Moving from information to revelation brought me out of religion and into relationship—a deep, loving, intimate relationship with the Lord. He wanted me to know His person, not just His principles. I surprisingly discovered that *He didn't want to be first in my life,* for then there would be a second and third vying for first place. My wife doesn't want to be the first woman in my life; she wants to be the only woman. Similarly, Jesus wants to be the only one thing in our life.

The process that moved me into that love relationship was highly transformational. Preaching and teaching are wonderful gifts in the body of Christ that feed our spirits and souls; however, it is not enough to live on other people's revelatory experiences. We must have our own. Most of my greatest transformational revelations came in times of waiting before the Lord, experiencing His majesty in creation, peering into His Word and hungering for the reality of what I was reading. Conflict was eliminated when He rewired me from knowing Him from the outside in to knowing Him from the inside out—that is, He changed my knowing center from my head to my spirit, from head knowledge to revelational knowledge, from knowing by my experiences or input from the world outside me to knowing Him by seeing and experiencing Him in my spirit.

It is important to note here that I know Him first by genuine trust and faith in His Word, despite my personal experience, and second, by revelation of His Word. The majority of my revelations have had nothing to do with what I should be doing or what I expected Him to do. For the most part, my revelations didn't answer any of my questions. Simply, but with great impact, He would open the eyes of my spirit to see who He is. This is an exciting, ongoing process. Seeing His goodness, His glory, His attributes—Jesus in all He is, all He did, and all He will do—is a never-ending adventure. It has become the foundation of my walk with the Lord. When everything else is brought into question, my default now is who He is as He has revealed Himself to me through His Word.

Job had a similar experience. Despite all his losses and all the questions he wanted answered, when the Lord broke in to speak to Job, He answered none of his questions but in extraordinary ways revealed *who He was*. The Lord asked Job "Who is this [meaning Job] that obscures my counsel without [revelational] knowledge?" Then the Lord revealed His glory to Job. Job then said, "Surely I spoke of things I did not understand, things too wonderful for me to know. My

> *The process Job went through changed his information about God to a personal revelation of God.*

ears had heard of you but now my [spiritual] eyes have seen you" (Job 42:3–5). The process Job went through changed his information about God to a personal revelation of God. The revelation transformed him forever. He was convinced.

Because of this process I have gone through, I am convinced that nothing can stop the love that God has for me; He who began a good work in me is faithful, and He will complete it. He is my good, good Father who loves me and created me to know His love. He is totally good, totally powerful, totally sovereign, and totally in control of bringing about His good will in my life and in the world. He works all things in my life together for my good. He is totally wise and knows what He's doing. He works in me with amazing grace and tender loving-kindness. He is totally in charge of my life, and I am convinced I can trust Him. He is the process initiator, who has always been there, watching over me when I made a mess in His kitchen. He is the God of the fried and will bring me through to well-done. God's sovereignty, power, and goodness are my security. God's wisdom is my comfort, and His love is my life.

I am convinced that it is God's deepest desire that we not merely know about Him and remain conflicted from worldly sources and life's experiences, but that we know Him intimately with full faith in His Word, enhanced by personal revelation. He wants us absolutely convinced in who He is. Knowing Him for who He is leads us to the next process.

Process 4: From Forgiven to Forgiving and Beyond

Experiencing God's love is the prerequisite to being convinced you are forgiven. Being forgiven is the prerequisite to healing. Healing is often completed by forgiving yourself and others. His love gives the capacity to forgive. Healing cannot take place without forgiveness, and forgiveness cannot take place without knowing the love of God.

Having worked hard for many years at becoming a fried Christian, when I finally arrived, I had many questions and many whys. Why did this happen to me? Why did people I loved and worked closely with betray and hurt me? Where was God in all of this? Where was the justice? Was there restitution for what was stolen? Would there ever be an apology for what they did? Would they ever be punished? The anger, broken-heartedness, and depression locked me up inside for a very long time until the Lord broke in and changed me with His love and forgiveness.

My comments here are by no means all there is to understand about forgiveness and love. It is a simple summary of what I experienced and learned through this process.

Unforgiveness keeps us tied to the past, bound to the offense and to the people who offended us. Thoughts and emotions meditated on and replayed over and over and over, keep the wound alive, driving it deeper into the soul. When we are in a state of unforgiveness, the offense continues to poison our entire being like a festering wound or a hidden cancer, developing bitterness and infecting every area of our lives negatively. It destroys the capacity for healthy relationships with God and others. Unforgiveness blocks the ability to be healed, to be free, and to move into a healthy future. The effects of unforgiveness are like a virus that cannot be contained, easily infecting others around you.

The future of relationships with those who have offended us is in our hands, the hands of the offended. For me, these potential future relationships included not only my offenders, but also God and others that I wanted to love. As offended as I was, I was crippled in having a healthy relationship with God. The bitterness of my soul infected the love I had for Him. My condition conflicted with His nature of love, forgiveness, and compassion. When the Lord broke into my dark night of the soul, He unconditionally loved me, asking nothing in return. I came to understand that all of my offenses against Him had been forgiven. I was astutely aware that He was totally holy and had every right to judge me for my offenses against Him. But He didn't. He forgave me, removing the offenses that stood between us.

As I grew in His love, *I realized that the offenses of others against me were insignificant in comparison to my offenses against Him,* a holy and loving God. He made it clear that He was the only righteous judge, and that judging others was playing God. I had no right to play judge, jury, and executioner. He lovingly removed me from the judgment seat and set me on the mercy seat. He showed me that the offenses committed against me were offenses against Him, and that He had forgiven them even as He had forgiven me. He left me with no option but to forgive them. I chose to forgive my offenders, one person at a time, one incident at a time.

Then He moved me beyond forgiveness to love. He challenged me from Matthew 5:44 that if I wanted to be His son, then I must love my enemies. Desiring to be a good son more than anything else, I nevertheless wrestled with Him, realizing I had no love of my own for them in my heart. Finally, I surrendered, willing to love those who had hurt me. I asked Him to put the love I needed in my heart. I soon discovered that the love He deposited in me was so great that it had the capacity to love my enemies even as He loved them. Receiving God's love and forgiveness for myself, and forgiving and loving others in His love, set me free.

Through this process, the Lord also realigned my understanding in the area of trust and loving others. He told me I must trust God and love man. To trust is to have a firm reliance on the integrity, ability, or character of a person or thing; it is having confident faith in a person or thing. The only person we should totally trust to meet our deepest needs is the Lord. He is the only one who can. He alone is totally trustworthy.

> *He told me I must trust God and love man.*

Scripture never tells us to put that kind of trust in man. Trusting man, including ourselves, to meet needs only God can meet is a trap and will always lead to disappointment and hurt. Misplaced trust in anyone or in anything other than the Lord leads to shattered dreams and destroyed hopes that cause the heart to become sick, discouraged, depressed, and hopeless. Trust in the Lord, however, produces hope, and hope fulfilled produces joy.

Hope that produces joy will spring up when our trust is in the Lord, not in man.

Tempered trust measured out to those people who have proven worthy allows us to maintain a healthy relationship with others without expecting them to meet our deepest needs. This leaves lots of room for us to forgive others but does not leave us empty and wounded when they fail to meet our expectations. Why? Because we've trusted God to meet our most fundamental needs and loved others in their inability to do so. Trust God, love others. Proverbs 3:5 says, "Trust in the Lord with all of your heart," and in John 13:34, Jesus said, "A new command I give you: love one another. As I have loved you, so you must love one another."

Joy then becomes the litmus test for how much we are trusting the Lord, experiencing His presence, and enjoying His pleasures.

Psalm 103 describes this love as loving-kindness and tender mercy. First Corinthians 13 highlights the full spectrum of the kind of love God is looking for from us. This realignment helps us to love others by seeing them as the Lord sees them. He sees our fallen nature, our brokenness, woundedness, imperfections, and our complete incapacity to save ourselves, yet He has compassion on us. From the cross, Jesus asked the Father to forgive us because He understood we don't know what we're doing. We don't have the capacity to do the right thing in ourselves. It's easier to forgive when we have compassion for the fallen condition of both ourselves and others.

In this process, *He also showed me how to discern between a broken person and a deceitful devil,* to identify the source behind the wound and how it played out in my life. He taught me to first forgive people and then charge the devil. Behind fallen mankind is a horde of demons that uses imperfect people to hurt other people. The devil finds it even easier to use those with wrong motives or evil in their heart. The devil also deceives and seduces well-meaning people who have right motives but lack wisdom and grace for reconciliation. Often playing on their wounds and immaturity, the enemy deceives "good people" into believing lies. Thinking they are acting righteously to bring about God's will, they are empowered with a divisive spirit and become like him, an irreconcilable accuser. God's love in Jesus has forgiven all men at the Cross, desiring to draw them to Himself and condemning the devil to hell. Crucified in Christ, we possess the same love that Jesus has for people. We are therefore to love people who are in or out of the kingdom, and war against our real enemy: the devil, the liar, the accuser of the brethren, and the enemy of reconciliation.

I have also found it comforting to understand that in every offense God is totally in control. Joseph had his brothers, David had Absalom, and Jesus had Judas. God uses what the enemy means for evil to bring about His plan: transformation into His image and the advancement of His

> *The cross shows us what that love looks like: a laid-down life expecting nothing in return, the unconditional surrender of self for the sake of another.*

plan of salvation. Every offense is an opportunity to trust in the Lord that He is working all things together for our good and His purposes.

Don't hesitate, communicate. As believers, we should never hesitate to go immediately to a brother or a sister where there is an offense and communicate the desire to be reconciled. The greatest hidden sin in the church is possibly not adultery, fornication, or abortion, but not obeying the command of the Lord in Matthew 5:23 to go to a brother or sister immediately if there is any offense between you and them. That applies in marriages, families, churches, and in our workplaces. Too often, however, we either bury the offense, seek agreement from others for our side of the issue, build a consortium against the other party, slander the person involved, or gossip about the situation.

Acting in these ungodly ways creates a toxic atmosphere that releases a demonic, divisive spirit that separates us from God and one another. *Without a sincere attempt to go directly to an offended or offending person in order to give and receive forgiveness, all other communications with them are charades, dishonest, and religious lies.* If we want to be a well-done lover of God, we must go directly to a brother or sister when there is an offense and seek reconciliation. We must repent for the times we have violated this scriptural directive. The Lord may very well direct us to go to those who have offended us or to those who are holding an offense against us to seek forgiveness and reconciliation.

It is important to note that this process of forgiveness and reconciliation is not a one-prayer, one-size-fits-all activity. It is specific and individual to each offense. It often takes many acts of forgiveness and actions toward reconciliation until the sting of the offense is gone and the relationship has been healed. During this process, He directed me to go to many people to ask for forgiveness for offenses I had committed against them. He also gave me the grace to forgive everyone He brought to my remembrance, who had offended me. However, He made it very clear that it was not my job to inform others of the offenses they had committed against me. *It is strictly the Holy Spirit's job to both convict of offenses committed against us and give the offender the grace to ask for forgiveness.*

Following His directives, I watched in astonishment as people contacted me, sometimes ten and fifteen years after an incident, and ask me to forgive them. Since I had already forgiven them, those were times of precious exchange and reconciliation. But let me tell you one amazing story. In the sixth grade, a group of boys at my school banded together under the leadership of a boy I will call "Charlie." They didn't like me. On several occasions, they chased me, surrounded me, and attempted to beat me up. Their harassment got so bad that my father had to get involved and go to Charlie's father. Just seven years ago, almost sixty years later, I received a letter in the mail asking if I was the Dennis Bambino who went to Pine Avenue Elementary School. If I was, the letter said, please call. It was signed Charlie.

Needless to say, I called immediately. Charlie got right to the point and asked me to forgive him for what he did

> *The path to becoming a well-done lover of God is paved with forgiveness.*

to me back in the sixth grade. He also desired to ask my father for forgiveness, but my father had already passed away. Since then, Charlie and I have become the best of friends. I have visited with him and stayed at his home. We have shared stories and laughed about the good old days. The Holy Spirit is amazing. Forgiveness always brings healing and reconciliation.

Process 5: From Reorientation to Re-Formation and Re-Definition

It is God's deepest desire to re-form us into the image and likeness of Jesus. For that to happen, He has to bring us through a process of reorientation. By that I mean He has to show us by revelation that when we were born again by His Spirit, He changed the way we relate to Him and the world. Through our rebirth, He radically shifted the control center of our being. Our body (with its sin-soaked appetites) and our soul (unrenewed mind, rebellious will, and damaged emotions) are no longer in control of who we are, what we think, and what we do. We are no longer subject to living according to the information, experiences, and words coming from the world outside us through the five senses of the body. No longer are we compelled to live from the outside in. Our regenerated spirit, in which Jesus and the Holy Spirit dwell, is now the control center of our being and the source of all truth and life.

This radical, even revolutionary, reorientation from living from the outside in to living from the inside out took place immediately at the new birth when we received Jesus as our Lord and Savior. Jesus, our conquering king, through His death, burial, and resurrection, purchased us and seated Himself at the center of our spirit as our new owner, king, and supreme ruler. He then filled our cleansed spirit with His Holy Spirit. This is the reorientation that shifts our center from our body and soul to our spirit. These first acts of reorientation begin the process of re-formation.

Although the Lord assumes the throne of our spirit at the time of salvation, the kingdom of darkness still illegally squats in our body and soul and must be expelled. From within our spirit center, the Lord starts to depose all other rulers until He is the only Lord of our life. This is the re-formation process in which the Lord destroys every usurping power in our body, soul, and spirit; heals every wound incurred before He was Lord; changes our mind-sets; destroys every lie and sets in the truth; renews our mind aligning it with His mind; and trains our will to choose His will. He fills our spirit with His Spirit to empower us to war and win against every invading spirit from the outside world that attempts to repossess us. This re-formation changes us from living out of the flesh to living by the Spirit. I received a prophetic word once that I needed a lobotomy, to get out of my head and to live out of my spirit. But I didn't know how to do that. You can't think it into being. It happens through a continuing process of revelational experiences.

The re-formation process produces re-definition of identity. It destroys the identity of being a separated sinner living outside the Lord's presence, to an abiding son or daughter living in His presence and His presence living in us; from being a worker striving to gain God's approval by changing themself from the outside in, to resting in His love and watching Him work the transformation from the inside out. According to Romans 8, this ongoing process is called "the law of the Spirit of life in Christ Jesus that set us free from the law of sin and death." The process will continue until we are conformed to the likeness of Jesus. This is the process of learning to live in the Spirit that I call "living inside out." Living from the outside in produces a fried Christian, but living inside out will transform you into a well-done lover of God.

Process 6: From Laborer to Lover

This is a core process to transform us into a well-done lover of God. In this process the Lord doesn't change who we are from the outside in by correcting what we do or how we do it (that's religion), but it converts our inner being, our nature, to be one with God's nature of love; that is, to become Christlike. Then out of who we are, a new creation in Christ, comes good works that bring Him glory. As God once told me, *I am changing you to be what you've never been so you can do what you've never done.* As I shared in "My Story, Part II," the Lord began this reorientation process in me after I quit and surrendered to Him, completely fried. After He caught me in my free fall into darkness, He asked me, *When did the Great Commission supersede the Great Commandment?* He had to reorient me to loving Him first and making Him my one thing. Then out of that love would flow a love for others and a natural obedience to keep His commands. Since then, in many times of great intimacy, He has revealed His extraordinary love for me. These revelational experiences created a growing response of overwhelming love for Him.

This process of becoming Christlike takes place as we come into the fullness of His love. John 15:9 and 17:21–23 tell us that Jesus loves us as much as the Father loves Him, and the Father loves us as much as He loves His Son, Jesus. That is mind-blowing. The Father and the Son love us as much as they love one another. Ephesians 3:17–19 explains that we need to be rooted in and built on this love. It is the core of everything we are and the foundation of our lives. The fullness of that love is found in union with the person of Jesus. The process of becoming a well-done lover of God causes us to know all the dimensions of the love of Christ, the width and length and height and depth of His love. We will experience His love, and *know this love,* which surpasses all knowledge.

This love is incomprehensible and cannot be grasped with the mind. It can only be known through a revelation of the Spirit. Knowing this love by revelational experience is the only way to become a valid messenger of the good news that the Father loves the world and sent His Son to bring lost sons and daughters back to Himself. Experiencing this love radically transforms us. This conversion ultimately changes our outer actions, by primarily transforming our nature in the very core of our being. We become, by a work of the Spirit, the visible image of Christ in us, converted from servant to son, from sinner to saint, from worker to worshiper, from laborer to lover, and from being driven to perform to resting in His presence. To end up a well-done lover of God, we must learn to cease from our striving and enter the rest of His finished work. Our identity then will no longer be in what we do, but in our love union with who Jesus is in us and who we are in Him. He makes His love so real in us that we are absolutely assured that we are approved sons and daughters loved by our Father.

Just as it was with Jesus, it will be with us. The Father loved and approved Jesus as His Son before He performed any miracles, preached any sermons, or completed His mission to die on the Cross. One of God's goals for us is that we live in the reality that we are no longer slaves driven to work at fulfilling His commands in order to gain His approval.

What does it look like to be converted from a laborer into a lover in union with Jesus? The Spirit opens our eyes to see in God's Word what we are to become. Jesus gives a perfect picture in John 15, the story of the vine and the branches, of the organic love union He has purposed for us. This union will produce much fruit (God's work, God's way, emanating God's nature). Producing much fruit is the equivalent of the branches (us) accomplishing their purpose and receiving a "well done." The key word in these scriptures is the same Greek word used twelve times and translated "abide," "remain" and "continue." In these verses, God showed me a mutual abiding, a life union, with the branch in the vine and the vine in the branch. Scripture emphasizes that the first and most essential activity of the branch is to abide in the vine, *not to produce fruit*. Fruit production is not a work of the branch to be accomplished

> *In Christ, we are loved sons and daughters preapproved by our good, good Father. We work out of approval, not for approval.*

on its own. Jesus says that without Him (without an intimate relationship with Him), we can do nothing.

The vine causes its life to produce fruit from the branch. The branch cannot work apart from the vine and expect to produce fruit. If the branch attempts to produce fruit without first abiding in the vine, it will fail. The branch will wither, die, and be cut off from the life of the vine. The fruit, then, results from the life of the vine in union with the branch. To produce fruit, the priority of the branch must be to become one with the vine. Our primary purpose is for us to become one with Jesus, love Him with all our heart, abide in Him, and live out of Him. Scripture tells us we do that by surrendering to His Word and His life abiding in us. This forms a vine–branch love union. Then His life through us naturally produces fruit to His glory and our joy. We rest in Him; He works through us.

The Lord showed me that the fruit produced is the life of the vine in another form. The branch is transformed and gives a fleshly body to the fruit. Mature fruit is Christ in us transformed. We are transformed into the body of Christ, thus becoming the visible image of who He is in us. Hungry people come to the vine for the fruit. They will come to us to taste and see the goodness of the Lord. The Word of God dwelling in us is the incorruptible seed of Christ. His Word, when received and believed, will reproduce His life in the consumer.

Jesus then emphasized that we must remain in His love. He tells us we will remain in His love if we obey His commands to love one another. As a worker, I strove to keep His commands as my primary activity, and that led to my becoming fried. I now realize that loving others and taking the good news of His gospel to the ends of the earth are the organic, natural results of abiding in Him. Love produces obedience. Merely being obedient doesn't mean that we love. Without love, obedience can be an act of legalism and religion. Parents and pastors who raise up children and churches to be obedient without love in the relationships produce people with a fear of punishment, a need for approval or affirmation, a desire for reward and acclamation, or even a fear of intimacy.

The elder son, in Luke 15:28–32, bragged of his obedience, describing himself as a slave. He obviously had no love relationship with his father, was filled with anger, and had no joy. In stark contrast, out of a love relationship with His Father, Jesus conceded His will to the Father's will, and for the joy set before Him endured the cross. When a teacher, disciple or parent has not been transformed by the love of God, they can reproduce nothing more than religious robots. Robots reproduce robots but cannot produce lovers.

Any lack of loving others, any lack of the fruit of love, is a sure sign of a lack of mutual abiding, our abiding in His love and receiving His love abiding in us.

"If you love Me" precedes "obey my commands." Loving Jesus and experiencing His love come first. Any lack of loving others, any lack of the fruit of love, is a sure sign of a lack of mutual abiding, our abiding in His love and receiving His love abiding in us. I discovered that it's easier to minister than to love, easier to obey than to love, and easier to serve than to love.

Above all, the Lord desires for us to produce much fruit, which will bring great joy. This is fruit that remains. Any fruit that has reproduced itself in another person will remain forever. Therefore, Jesus's command to love is a call to deeply abide. It is a call to life union with Jesus. Like the sheep in Matthew 25:31–45, who weren't aware of the good they had done, obedience becomes an oblivious, organic action of our Christlike nature that we received when we were born again. On the other hand, the goats, out of their unregenerate separated nature, were oblivious to not doing the good they should have done.

The sheep, though just as oblivious as the goats, automatically went out and did good without even being asked. We, the sheep of His pasture, will do the will of God out of a desire to love the one who extravagantly loves us. We do not love because we are obedient. That could easily be religious performance, being obedient to the letter of the law without love in our heart. We are obedient because we love. Obedience is the fruit of love. Loving the Lord our God with our whole heart, mind, soul, and strength, making Him our first thing, causes a love for others to flow from us. Loving Him compels us to take that love to all the world. This process will not end until we are well-done lovers of God.

> *This is the Father's purpose for us: a love union that transforms us into the image and likeness of His beloved Son, Jesus, and reproduces His love in others.*

As I've said, "If you love Me" precedes "keep my commandments." The Great Commandment, to love the

Lord, and the second commandment like it, to love others, precedes the Great Commission. Obedience, therefore, to love one another, to produce fruit, and to take this gospel to the whole world is a command to love the Lord first. No striving, no stress, no fear of failure—just abiding. Abide in a Lord-and-lover union. Isn't this how children are birthed? Union precedes and then produces procreation. The process of producing a well-done lover of God is a labor of love by the Spirit, not a work of the flesh by us.

Process 7: From Hurt to Healing

Without the ongoing processes of seeing and experiencing who God is, receiving and releasing forgiveness, and experiencing His profound love, it is impossible to be totally healed and made whole.

He created a vacuum in us that only He can fill. I can trace all my wounds to seeking fulfillment of these basic needs in things or other people. In every case, they failed to fulfill me, leaving me empty and wounded. But I have experienced a continuing revelation of God's love in Christ. These relational experiences have healed the wounds and filled the vacuum. Ephesians 3:19 tells us we can "know this love that surpasses knowledge that you may be filled to the measure of all the fullness of God." This is a deeply personal

> *The basic needs of a person to be loved, to be secure, to have identity, to be recognized, and to be accepted can only be satisfied in a love relationship with the Lord.*

process that takes place in your intimate time with the Lord. Experiencing His love causes you to feel totally safe and secure. Then He opens the coffins of your heart to exhume emotions and pain that have been buried alive.

Isaiah 61:1 speaks of Jesus, who was "sent to bind up the brokenhearted, to proclaim freedom for the captives and release from darkness for the prisoners." Psalm 34:18 says, "The Lord is close to the brokenhearted and saves those who are crushed in spirit." He will gently lead you to the cross. There, by revelation, He will show you the Father's Lamb who took your place, bore all your grief, carried all your sorrow; the Lamb who was despised, rejected, and abandoned. There, by His substitutionary beatings, abuses, and pain, you are healed. In Christ crucified, we are set free, forgiven, healed, and delivered of all the pain of the past. During this process, I had a vision of Christ's bleeding body on the Cross. I stood before the cross as a dark gray figure. Then, as I moved closer and closer, it was as if I were absorbed and disappeared into His body. I knew intuitively that when He died, I died in Him. All my sin died, all my pain died, all my past died. I died.

> *I understand now that we cannot be victorious warriors or effective ministers of His gospel of love with hidden, bleeding, pain-filled wounds.*

Immediately after, in the same vision, I saw Christ exploding forth from the tomb. Then, out of His radiant, glorious body, I emerged, brand-new and filled with light. I was alive in the risen Christ. Revelation like this makes His healing love a reality. We must be healed in our soul, mind, and emotions. Hurt people hurt people. Healed people heal people. After Jesus rose from the dead, He showed Himself to His disciples. In His glorified body, He bore the marks of the wounds He had received. But they were not bleeding. There was no pain—they were healed. Jesus told Thomas to put his fingers in His nail-pierced hands and put his hand into the wound in His side. Jesus told him to stop doubting and to believe. Thomas's response was "My Lord and my God." The marks of Jesus's healed wounds were a testimony to the effective work of the cross to bring healing and the power of the resurrection to bring new life. We also will carry the marks of our own wounds. However, once healed, our wounds become a living testimony of the power of the Lord's death and resurrection, bringing hope to the despondent, faith to doubters, healing to other unhealed wounded warriors, and worship to our Lord.

Process 8: From Failure to Formation

In my life, I had always struggled with the need to succeed. Actual failure and perceived failure for not being perfect kept me under condemnation and a lot of pressure. Feeling like a failure separated me from other people and from the Lord. During this process, the Lord's love broke through and showed me the difference between sin and failure. There is a big difference between the two. Simply put, sin is willful disobedience while failure is not achieving an expected end, i.e. being perfect. While there is often sin in failure, failure is not sin. The Lord uses failure to expose the roots that are causing it; then He destroys the roots. Failure rooted in pride, rebellion, self-will, and disobedience calls for repentance. Failure rooted in foolishness, lack of maturity, or believing lies, along with the need to succeed rooted in the need for approval, acceptance, love, recognition, and security, calls for radical changes in the way we think and believe, as well as a revelational encounter with the love of God.

Failure teaches us about our weaknesses and the need to totally rely upon God's strength, mercy, and grace. The Lord uses failure to bring us to a place of conviction, absolute surrender, and total humility, thus allowing Him to completely take over and live in us and through us. He uses failure to form us into the image of Christ, to humble us but never to humiliate us, to convict us but never to condemn us, to discipline us but never demean or degrade us, and to conquer us with his kindness until we are yielded to the Father's will. This process taught me that, in Christ, although we have failed, we are not failures. Though we have sinned, we are not sinners. We are imperfect sons and daughters perfectly loved by our Father. In this relationship, we are corrected and disciplined by love, not by punishment. He believes in us, restores us, and uses our failures as life lessons to bring us into His plan for our lives. Confessing both our sin and weakness to the Lord brings us into a place of abiding in His forgiveness and grace. There, standing

> *Failure is the unavoidable experience the Lord uses in the lives of Christians to perfect them in His love and transform them into His image.*

unashamed in His presence, we thank Him for our sonship. Secure in our sonship, there is no fear of failure, no fear of punishment.

If we are afraid to fail at doing anything, we will probably succeed at doing nothing. Fear of punishment will keep us from coming to the Father for all we need to succeed. Those fears, however, are dissolved in God's perfect love. Experiencing God's love frees us to fail in the process of becoming perfect. I've learned to keep my heart focused on the Lord, while not presuming on His love or taking license from it to be negligent. I seek always to please His heart, knowing that I will fail to be perfect. Nonetheless, I am secure in knowing that the Father's perfect love for me never fails.

I have allowed my failures to teach me. In the face of failure, we can either break down or break through. We can run from the Father or run to Him. We can stand in pride, defend ourselves, make excuses, shift blame, or beat ourselves up and sink into a state of self-hatred and depression for failing to be perfect. In contrast, we can humble ourselves, confess our weaknesses to God, receive His forgiveness, forgive ourselves, and grow through the process. Learning from my failures has been transformational; it has changed me deeply. Failed, forgiven, and re-formed is my testimony, the testimony of a maturing son of God.

Here are some additional points to help move you from failure to formation:

- To move forward today into your tomorrows, you must resolve your yesterdays.

- Fail forward, learning and being transformed by every experience. Thoroughly process every event, hurt, and failure. Then move on.
- Do not build a memorial to past negative experiences, continually going back to visit them. They will hold you hostage. Instead, tear them down.
- Confess your sonship. Who you are in Christ defines you, not what happened in the past.
- Forgive yourself, forgive others, and then love yourself and love others.
- Renounce self-pity, defeat, and failure.
- Listen closely for His still, small voice, be obedient to what you hear, and you will always be in His perfect will.

Process 9: Fire for Refining

To become a well-done lover of God, we cannot avoid the furnace of affliction and the fire of adversity. The God I've come to know is a loving Father. He allows and orchestrates trials, testings, and persecutions, working all of them together for our refining. His objective is not to see us fail, but rather to strengthen our strengths and shore up our shortcomings. For example, Jesus told Peter in Lk.22:31 that the devil had requested to sift him like wheat, but He had prayed for him. He also told Peter that he would be restored and used to strengthen others. Jesus was totally aware of Peter's upcoming testing but did not stop what was necessary to refine him. Strength is built through resistance, and purification is achieved through fire. In what is called the Hall of Faith, in Hebrews, chapter 11, we read of the great men and women of God who endured severe trials, testings, and persecutions to perfect their faith. Just as they became a trophy of grace, so it will be with us.

There are three analogies that have helped me better understand this process:

Purification by Fire

Gold and silver, precious metals, are placed into a crucible and heated until they boil. The impurities that bubble to the surface are skimmed off by the blacksmith. The blacksmith keeps the metals in the fire until he can see his image in them. He desires what is precious to him to be pure, maximizing its value in the marketplace. The Father loves us, and we are precious to Him. He will use the fires of adversity to purge out every impurity until He sees the image of His Son, Jesus, in us. Then we will be well-done, maximizing our value in the Father's plan to redeem an unsaved world by reflecting Jesus.

Fire for Finishing

Potters form clay vessels into images pleasing to them. They put the molded vessels in a kiln and turn up the heat. In the heat of the kiln, the vessel is solidified and made firm. The potter's unique design is baked forever into the clay. The skill of a master potter is amazing. Each vessel, unique in its dimensions, must stay in the heat for a perfect period of time. If taken out too soon, it will be only half-baked. It will fall apart because it is not strong enough to fulfill its appointed purpose. If left too long in the heat, it will crack, become fried—a cracked pot, if you will—and crumble under pressure. How does the master potter know when to take the vessel out? He listens with a skilled ear for the vessel to ping, or as they say in the trade, "sing in the fire." He then quickly pulls it out. It is well-done, ready for the master's use.

The application is obvious. Each of us is formed as a unique vessel by the hands of the Lord. We will be tried by fire to make sure we are solid and strong, able to fulfill the specific purposes He has ordained us for. We are to be vessels with the fulness of the Holy Spirit in us and yielded to the Holy Spirit being poured out from us. Vessels not perfectly fired will crack and fall apart under the pressure of the powerful ministry of the Holy Spirit in us and through us and the vicious attacks of the enemy against us. They will not have the strength or courage to prevail in the heat of battle. Therefore, the Master Potter will wait until we sing His praises in the fire of adversity, knowing then that we completely trust Him and fully surrender to His will. Now, precisely at the right time, the Master Potter will take us out of the fire, a well-done vessel, formed in His image to fulfill His purposes.

Testings for Approval

Electrical products have a sticker on them that says "UL approved" or "conforms to UL standards." This emblem signifies that the product has undergone rigorous tests in a lab. These tests assure both the manufacturer and the ultimate purchaser that the product performs to the intended design and purposes of the manufacturer and will meet the needs of the purchaser, thus producing a satisfied customer. If the product fails any of these tests or fries under pressure, it is not discarded but sent back to the manufacturer to perfect its weakness. Then it goes back to the lab for more testing until it performs to the manufacturer's specifications. Finally, the product receives a stamp of approval and is ready to be sent into the world market to deliver services to ultimately satisfied customers.

The product represents the manufacturer in the marketplace. A satisfied customer will come back for more products from that manufacturer and tell others of its products. If the product does not undergo the testing process in the lab and goes to market unproven, when it fails under the pressure to meet needs as advertised, it will produce a dissatisfied, even angry, customer. This disgruntled customer may never come back to that manufacturer again; he will likely go to other manufacturers and most likely will communicate his dissatisfaction to others.

Again, the applications are obvious. The Lord wants to test us in a controlled environment until we have been perfected in the design and function He created us to be in, even the image of Jesus, and received His approval for service. Then, when we go into the world to represent Him, we will be able to deliver the character and ministries of Jesus to multitudes who are looking for the Christ in us to meet their deepest needs.

It is important to understand that this stamp of approval is for service; there is a difference between approval for service and the Father's love and approval for us as His children. We are always loved by our Father as His children, whether untested, in testing, or perfected. We do not need to perform to gain His love and approval. We are preapproved *as His child*.

Approved sons and daughters are tested to mature their ability to complete their purpose. This can be seen clearly in the life of Jesus. In Matt.3:16-17, the Father pronounced His love and approval over Jesus when He was baptized: "This is my Son, whom I love; with him I am well pleased." Jesus hadn't done anything to merit that approval. Then in Lk.4:1-2,14, the Holy Spirit led Him into the desert to be tested after which He came out well-done, empowered by the Holy Spirit and approved for service. He was ready to meet the needs of everyone who came to Him and complete the mission the Father had given Him.

> *We work out of approval, not for approval. Then we are proven through testings for service.*

Too many of us, myself included, have "rushed to market." We have pursued ministry, untried and unproven, only to fail, become fried, and bring disgrace to His name. Some of that may be the result of a combination of factors. First, we may not have had full revelatory knowledge of the fact that the Father loves us as His child and approves us without performance. Second, the zeal that consumed us may have driven us out too soon. We weren't sent out—we ran out to prove ourselves. And some of us were kicked out. Like fire outside the fireplace, zeal can burn the house down. Zeal must be released through character transformation.

Thank God we have a "manufacturer," a loving Father who does not discard us when we fail in the testing process. He loves us, gathers us back into a safe lab, and continues to refine us. For forty days after His resurrection,

Jesus did this with His disciples who had failed the test and crumbled in the crunch. He loved them, but they weren't yet ready for service. He is determined to perfect us to fulfill the calls and destinies upon our lives to reach a lost and dying world.

Last of all, many of us did not have time in a lab run by qualified specialists who themselves had been through testings and now took responsibility for mentoring others through the process. The absence of tested fathers in the faith has caused too many untested and unapproved—albeit well-intentioned—servants to run out, drop out, fall out, or get kicked out into the marketplace only to fail in public. The value of the master-apprentice, father-son, mother-daughter relationship, cannot be understated. There is a great need for Moses–Joshua, Paul–Timothy, Mary-Joseph-Jesus relationships to raise up the next generation of tested leaders. Local churches, Bible schools, ministries, and families must become "safe labs" with the primary purpose of processing and maturing the sheep under their care. Testing them for service, we can send them out as approved saints of God to do the works of ministry (Eph. 4:11–16).

Surrendering to the Lord of the process accelerates the refining, reducing the time in process until we are released to go into the world. To look like Jesus, we need only to look at Jesus. To be Christlike, we need only to see what Christ was like in His earthly ministry. Who was He, and what did He do through His trials, testings, and persecutions for Him to finish well-done? On every level and with the highest degree of intensity, Jesus was tried by fire. He was challenged to obey and submit to His parents at the age of twelve. He was confronted with forty days of temptation by the devil himself in every part of His being. He was continually attacked with false accusations and entrapments from religious leaders. He courageously walked through crowds attempting to murder Him, was accused of being demonized, abandoned by His followers and disciples, rejected by His family, and betrayed by one of His closest apostles. He sweat blood as He wrestled with His Father's will in Gethsemane and was then traded for a murderer, tortured and mutilated, condemned, and crucified as a criminal. Yet on the third day, He gloriously rose well-done.

How did Jesus pass through all these fires to come out as pure gold? He was always obedient to the Father's commands, trusting the Father to deliver Him. His will was to do the will of the Father, fearing God more than He feared man. He did not strive for the acceptance and approval of man, but remained steadfast in the love of His Father as Father's approved Son. He tenaciously held to God's Word. Jesus knew how to get into the secret place where He could see what the Father was doing and hear what the Father was saying. Jesus never capitulated to the circumstances, the people, the pain, or the pressure. He never moved in His own strength, but worked only by the power of the Holy Spirit. He continually demonstrated love in place of hate and compassion instead of judgment. He forgave His oppressors. He never quit until His mission was finished. Finally, surrendering only to the Father, He waited in faith for the fulfillment of the Father's promise to raise Him from the dead. Jesus is the perfect example of the testings the Father allows us to go through to produce a loved, approved and proven, well-done lover of God.

Process 10: The Father Factor: Orphan to Son

It is hard to rank in importance the processes already listed. But this last one is fundamental to them all. The Lord must be established as our primary, living Father, replacing the position of our earthly father. We must experience the Father's love and pleasure in us before we can grow in a love relationship with Him and be transformed into the image of His Son. It was necessary in the life of Jesus for Joseph, his father here on earth, to pass away and for His heavenly Father to take His place as Jesus's primary, living father. At Jesus's baptism, Joseph was already gone. God the Father firmly established Himself as Jesus's everlasting Father and acknowledged Jesus as His Son, whom He loved and was pleased with. Jesus received His identity as a son and experienced the Father's pleasure in Him before He ever performed a miracle or preached a sermon. This transition secured the identity of Jesus in the Father's love.

Jesus's new identity as the Father's Son became the most important reality of who He was and the foundation for everything He would do. Jesus's ministry and message from that point on was that God was His Father, He was the Father's Son, and they were one. Because it was so central to who Jesus was, it was the area of primary attack for the devil and the religious rulers. The devil tried to destroy Jesus's identity in the desert, challenging Him, "If you are the Son of God ..." The Pharisees hated Him not for what he did, but for His claim of being the Son of God. His identity was the reason they wanted Him crucified. Through every attack, however, Jesus was secure in knowing the Father loved Him and approved

Him, not for what He was doing, but for who He was as the Father's Son. Each of us must go through this process to become firmly established in our identity as a son or daughter of our Father God who loves us, takes pleasure in us, and approves us, not for anything we do or will ever do, but for who we are as the object of His love.

At seven years old, I played Little League baseball. My father was the coach of the team. He taught me how to pitch and put me on the mound in the first game. We won 22 to 2. At the last pitch, I ran off the mound to my father on the sidelines, expecting to be lifted up and celebrated. Instead, as I got within a few feet of him, he extended his arm with his hand up, stopping me from jumping into his arms, and said, "Not so fast. Next week is another game." Throughout my youth, if I got an 80 on a test, my father wanted to know why it wasn't a 100. If I got a 100, he wanted to know whether I got the extra points. In my high school yearbook, he wrote, "Aim high." No matter what I did, it was never enough, never good enough, and only mutely celebrated. The message was clear and deeply embedded in who I was: I would not be loved and accepted unless I was perfect.

I've since come to realize that my father was loving me in the best way he knew how to create in me a hard worker with a spirit of excellence. It did that. I became a hard worker at everything I did. I strove for excellence, but it was never enough and never good enough. Unfortunately, that belief carried over into my relationship with God. In my service to God, I never felt that I had done enough, that it was good enough, or that I was celebrated, loved, approved, and accepted by the Father.

Going from Spiritual Burnout to Well-Done Lover of God

Elder-Son Syndrome and Orphan Spirit

As I went through this process, the Lord showed me that in feeling unapproved by the Father, I had taken on the elder-son syndrome of Luke 15:25-32 and become infected with an orphan spirit. Together these form the identity of a person who feels parentless, abandoned, rejected, marginalized, invisible, separated, labeled, and homeless. Such a person feels he must work for and defend everything he needs. The orphan strives to make a place for himself, win affection, get attention, and be noticed. He strives for status, works for security, and labors to earn relationships, but he never feels accepted, appreciated, approved, and valuable for who he is.

Sonship

Identity founded in a revelation that God is your Father and you are His child, and that He loves you, takes pleasure in you, and approves you destroys all other lying identities. You come to know that your identity, who you are, is *not* founded on the following: It is:

- Not based on what you do: achieving accomplishments, promotions, awards, degrees, or accolades;
- Not based on your status: being rich or poor, influential or not, or the bearer of titles and authority;
- Not based on possessions: having money, houses, cars, or stuff;
- Not based on occupations and callings: being a laborer or lawyer, pastor or president, mogul or mother;

- Not based on attributes: possessing certain gifts, talents, or character traits;
- Not based on conditions: being sick or healthy, strong or weak, pretty or plain, high IQ or low, young or old;
- Not based on responses from other people: being loved, respected, and accepted, or being despised and rejected; and
- Not based on secondary relationships: being a son or daughter, husband or wife, mother or father, brother or sister, or having a large number of friends.

What is my identity? Who Am I?

I am who I am because the great I AM birthed me by the spirit to be exactly who I am. The I AM is love. Love created me in His image. The Creator fathered me. I am a child of His love. That is who I am—a loved child.

God is my loving Father. He loves me, approves me, and takes pleasure in me. What He created me to be is very good. I am not who I am because I did something, accomplished something, or worked for it. There is no striving to be his loved child, no competition, no perfection to be reached, no jealousy, no control, no comparisons in my being loved. I am uniquely, personally, singularly, tenderly crafted by love to be loved, to love Him. I am loved for who I am, the Father's child. That is who I am.

Where does this process take place? It happens in your renewed mind and in your spirit by revelation of the Holy Spirit based on God's Word. When does this process begin? It begins when you are born again and become a new creation in Christ Jesus. How often do you need the revelations of this process? You will need them many times, over and over, daily, even moment by moment, especially in the battle to protect your identity. The revelations of this process are your defense against every wicked thing that would draw you away from the goodness of your Father and the loving relationship He created you for. These revelations are your life in Christ.

My Strong Admonition

Stay in the processes the Lord is putting you through. Trust Him! He will be faithful to complete what He has begun. The pain is worth the finished product, the image of Christ. *Remember, you're not done until you're well-done.* Press in to His presence. Rest in His love while He works His love in you. He is the one who produces a well-done lover of God.

THE PLACES FOR BECOMING WELL-DONE

The places the Lord has used to accomplish His purposes in me are places where I am alone with Him: my regular quiet place at home, a walk with Him, a retreat away from home, and specific calls to fasting and prayer. Despite all the powerful impartations I've received from other preachers and teachers, church services, conferences, revival meetings, crusades, and prayer and worship meetings, the times alone with the Lover of my soul are the ones that have most radically changed me. My relationship with Jesus has grown from slavery to servanthood to friendship to a marital relationship.

In my marital relationship with my wife, Jackie, we serve one another continually, communicate throughout the day, and display regular signs of affection. However, one of the biggest keys to our fifty-three years of marriage has been making it a priority to have special times together: weekly dates and times of deep conversation and intimacy. Even when we were raising our family and faced with many demanding responsibilities, we would set aside time to be alone, to separate from all the busyness of life and focus on each other. Nothing and no one else were permitted to come with us into our secret place. We would have in-house dates in our den, putting up a curtain and telling the children they weren't allowed to trespass. (They constantly peeked to see what we were doing!)

My relationship with Jesus is now very much the same. I serve Him, communicate with Him continually throughout the day, and show Him public signs of affection through prayer, praise, thanksgiving, and worship. But the key to experiencing His love and presence is my entering the secret place, my dwelling place with Him and Him alone.

The Secret Place

The secret place is anywhere and anytime we separate ourselves to be alone with Jesus. This is where I find my salvation, my Savior, my life, my Lord, and my Lover. It is a holy place, my happy place, a resting place, a place of restoration, a safe place to be vulnerable and intimate. My secret place is like my living room with the Lord, where I sit on my Father's lap and we hang out as friends, enjoy casual conversation, and laugh together. It's like my kitchen, where we create new and wonderful things, where I feast at the table of the Lord, devouring His Word. It's like my bedroom, where I rest while He holds and comforts me, where we dream together. It is the place where I lay my head on Jesus's chest, open my heart to Him, hear His heartbeat, and feel His breath upon my head and face. It's the place where we are intimate and become one. It is the throne room where I experience His glory and majesty and worship Him with holy reverence and awe. It's the boardroom where I hear His plans and directives to build His kingdom, the war room where He releases strategies to overcome the enemy and give me my marching orders.

I enter my secret place most often through large doors of thanksgiving and praise—through the door of thanksgiving for all He has done and all He will do, and through the great door of praise as I exalt Him for all He is. I have had to expand my vocabulary with hundreds of words to expound His attributes and describe His character. I most often enter His presence through worship songs. There in His presence, the Spirit moves on me to pray, praise, worship, meditate on His Word, and very often to wait in silence, enjoy His presence, and listen expectantly for His voice.

Separation

The secret to the well-done life of Jesus was His continuous separation to be alone with the Father. Before ministry and after ministry, Jesus separated from the crowds, including His disciples, and went off to be alone with His Father. What He received during those times enabled Him to minister to people and overcome every attack of the enemy. In His intimate times with the Father, Jesus saw and heard in the Spirit. John 5:19 and 8:28 tell us He did only what He saw the Father do and said only what He heard the Father say. Out of Jesus's habitual and intentional separations came dynamite ministry.

I have found that we must be intentional and *choose* to separate from everything and everyone to be alone with Him. Choosing separation involves separating *from* something and separating *unto* something of greater value. We make decisions to separate all the time in life. We cannot accept job offers from more than one employer. To be successful, we must separate from all other opportunities and choose the one job we are going to put all our time and effort into. We cannot have a marital relationship with more than one person. To have a strong marriage, we must choose the one that we are to marry, separate from all other relationships, and make that person the first and only one in our life.

To be a well-done lover of God, there are strategic, appointed times when we must first, choose to separate from the world, its traditions and routines, its busyness and noise, the old normal, the familiar, addictive comforts, self-centered pursuits, and kingdom relationships and assignments. Second, we must choose to separate unto the Lord—shut out the world, go into our secret place, and spend quality time with Him. Choosing to separate daily is essential. Additionally, choosing extended times to go on retreats, to enjoy a honeymoon with the lover of your soul, deepens your relationship with the Lord and accelerates the processes He is bringing you through.

Separation is imperative. It is nonnegotiable in the continuing process of becoming a well-done lover of God.

Ten Powerful Purposes of Separation

Throughout Scripture, we see that the Lord has used times of separation to process His sons and daughters. These strategic separations transform His children into powerful, well-done lovers of God and launch them into His purposes for them.

*1. Separation Develops **Maturation**.*

Before He began to minister, Jesus grew in maturity during His separation from the public for thirty years. Scripture gives us a small window into His development at twelve years old. Luke 2:47 records, "Everyone that heard was amazed at his understanding and his answers ... and Jesus grew in wisdom and maturity and in favor with God and man." By revelation, Jesus grew to understand God's heart and ways. He developed a holy reverence for God, a personal knowledge of God as Father, and the call on His life to be about the Fathers business. Spending time with God and His Word, He became equipped to give answers to those seeking to know God or challenging God's Word. He received revelation of who He was and who God was. In His separation, He found favor with His good Father and came forth finding favor with man.

For us, chosen separations set us aside to become equipped in revelations from God's Word, revelations of the Father's love for us, and revelations of who we are in

Christ, who Christ is in us, as well as giving us multiple experiences of His goodness and wisdom and clarity on the specific call to serve Him. As we emerge from these chosen separations, we will have become secure in the Father's love for us, enabling us to bring God's power, wisdom, and answers to a dying and hostile world. He will also give us favor with the people to whom we are to reveal His love.

*2. Separation for **Purification** Prepares Us for **Intercession**.*

Purim is the Jewish feast that celebrates the story of Esther. She was chosen, separated, purified, and beautified to prepare her to go into the presence of the king. There she found favor with the king and became royalty, the queen (Est. 2:12). Faced with an impending threat to annihilate her people, she was counseled by Mordecai to go into the presence of the king and intercede for her people to be saved. He said, (Est. 4:14) "and who knows but that you have come to royal position for such a time as this?" Esther's separation for purification prepared her for a royal position of favor with the king. As royalty, she now held a place of strategic capacity to intercede for the deliverance of a people who were under a demonic threat of destruction.

During our times of chosen separation, the Lord will cleanse and purify us from everything that defiles our spirit, soul, or body. Extended separation times of fasting and prayer, one to seven days or longer, purges the lust of the flesh, the lust of the eyes, and the pride of life. Purified by the blood of Jesus we can confidently go into the presence of our God and King having the assurance in our hearts that we have the King's favor. Standing before the King in our royal position as the Bride of Christ we can beseech Him on behalf of other people.

Chosen separations renew our dedication, confidence, and courage to stand in intercession before the Lord between the enemies of His kingdom and people targeted by the enemy for destruction. In this way, we bring deliverance from the plots and plans of the evil one, shutting down the attacks of sickness, death, and destruction against ourselves, our family, and our nation and people groups around the world. As royal representatives of the King, we can stand in the gap to see captives set free and birthed into the kingdom. We have come to royal position to powerfully intercede for a one-billion-soul harvest. We are called to separation, purification, and intercession for such a time as this.

> *Purified by the blood of Jesus we can confidently go into the presence of the King having the assurance in our hearts that we have the King's favor.*

3. *Separation Becomes the Battleground for* **Confrontation** *That Results in* **Domination***.*

Luke 4:1 says, "Jesus, full of the Holy Spirit ... was led by the Spirit in the desert [a lonely separated wilderness] where for forty days He was tempted by the devil." Here He won domination over the world, the flesh, and the devil. Jesus's confrontations in this separation empowered Him with the Holy Spirit, as we read in Luke 4:14: "Jesus returned to Galilee in the power of the Holy Spirit."

Separation under the administration of the Holy Spirit progresses from being *filled* with the Holy Spirit to being *empowered* by the Holy Spirit. In strategic times of separation, we can confront our demons and all the deceptions and lies that attack our identity in Christ and aim to pull us out of the presence, power, and purposes of God. In a safe place with the Lord, under the administrations of the Holy Spirit, without condemnation or fear, we can become vulnerable. We can face our lack of love, besetting sins, inherited iniquity, unacceptable habits and tendencies, attitudes and character flaws. Using the Word of God as the sword of the Spirit as Jesus did, we can gain victory in these areas, come out from oppression under them, and dominate over them. We will then come forth in the power of the Holy Spirit to fulfill our destiny.

These Holy Spirit–led separations are as important for us as they were for Jesus. Nothing short of the power of the Holy Spirit is sufficient to meet the challenges we will face in a world moving swiftly into end-time scenarios. Nothing short of Holy Spirit power will win multitudes to the Lord.

4. *Separation Facilitates* **Rejuvenation**.

Song of Solomon 2:10 (emphasis added) reads, "My lover spoke and said to me, 'Arise, my darling, my beautiful one, and *come away with me.*'" The Spirit of the Lord beckons us to separate, arise from our doldrums, come aside, and come away to a separated place with Him. It is a call from our Lover to do the following:

- Renew our first love; be alone together; reaffirm our one thing, the only thing that is most

important, our love for the Lord; to be saturated in His lavish love;
- Renew our strength as we release thanksgiving, praise, prayer, and worship to the Lord;
- Be intimate with the Lord—unveiled, uncovered, and unashamed;
- Surrender all things to Him and experience the peace that passes all understanding; and
- Experience the joy of the Lord as His healing love removes all fears.

As we emerge from these come-away times with our lover Lord, we will have been changed. We will be closer to Him. However, we will re-enter a world that has also changed—a world moving further and further, faster and faster, away from Him. Therefore, we must continually change, growing more and more in love with Him, more and more transformed into His image.

5. *Separation Is the Environment of **Dedication** That Brings **Visitation**.*

Hannah dedicated Samuel to the Lord. In 1 Samuel 1:28, she said, "So now I give him to the Lord. For his whole life he will be given over to the Lord." Verse 21 of chapter 2 says, "…the boy Samuel grew up in the presence of the Lord" (separated).

To be a brighter light in the increasing darkness, a lavish lover in a hate-filled world, and a healing balm to hurting people, we must regularly come away with Him.

Chapter 3 continues the story: Samuel was lying down in the temple, alone, where the ark of God was. Then the Lord called Samuel by name and Samuel answered three times "Here I am" (vv. 3–8). "The Lord came and stood there, calling as at the other times, 'Samuel, Samuel.' Then Samuel said 'Speak, for your servant is listening'" (v. 10).

    E. M. Bounds has said that "prayer is the habit, the rule, of him who has dedicated himself fully to God. He who gives all to God will get all from God." (*The Power of Prayer*, E. M. Bounds, 2007 Christian Arts gifts).We need special times of separation to rededicate ourselves to the Lord for His purposes and to spend time in His presence, waiting upon Him to visit us, to call our name and speak. Dedicated separation tunes the ears of our heart to listen intently for His voice. It prepares us to be servants who will obey what we hear.

    We are in a critical time in history. We must have ears to hear what the Spirit is saying to the Church. Separation enables us to hear the voice of the Lord, the voice of the Spirit of Truth, loud and clear over the noise of the world. We must be the servants that the Lord knows are listening to Him and will obey.

6. *Separation Births* **Revelation**.

    Because of persecution, John was forcibly separated and totally isolated on the island of Patmos. John knew, however, that he was there because of the word of the Lord and the testimony of Jesus (Rev. 1:9). Even separations we have no control over will be used by the Lord. This was God's divinely orchestrated isolation to give John revelation.

So it is with us. We can separate ourselves to receive, through dreams, visions, and spiritual impartations, the word of the Lord. We can see and hear revelations from Jesus and of Jesus in all His glory. These fresh revelatory testimonies can then be shared with others to open their hearts to who He is and what He is about to do. As Revelation 1:1–3 (emphasis added) reads:

"The revelation of Jesus Christ, which God gave him to show his servants what must *soon* take place. He made it known by sending his angel ... who testifies to everything he saw—that is the word of God and the testimony of Jesus Christ. Blessed is the one who reads the words of this prophecy, and *blessed are those who hear it and take to heart what is written in it, because the time is near.*"

There is an urgency in the Spirit for us to separate and receive revelation. The Holy Spirit wants to equip us to see and hear by the Spirit what is happening and what is about to happen. Revelation 2:7, 11, 17, 29 and 3:6, 13, and 22 repeats a seven fold admonition: "He who has an ear, let him hear what the Spirit says to the churches." He wants to impart revelatory knowledge of His Word, both *logos* and *rhema*. He wants us to see Jesus in all of His glory as never before. If we will separate and listen, He will enable us to communicate these revelations to other servants of God who are also receiving revelation. Then He will embolden us to communicate these revelations to the world. These revelations will not only be visions of the coming glorious King, but also warnings of what is to come, worship in the heavens, wisdom for the future, and weapons of warfare for the saints.

Times of separation, whether imposed or voluntary, are designed to bring critical revelations for us, our families, the Church, and the world. We must hear what the Spirit is saying because the time is near.

7. *Separation Produces* **Declaration.**

John the Baptist was separated in a desert place to hear God and become the trumpet to boldly declare the first coming of the Lord:

"…the word of God came to John … *in the desert.* He went into all the country around the Jordon, preaching a baptism of repentance for the forgiveness of sins. As is written in the book of the words of Isaiah the prophet: "A voice of one calling in the desert, 'Prepare the way for the Lord, make straight paths for him. Every valley shall be filled in, every mountain and hill made low. The crooked roads shall become straight, rough ways smooth. And all mankind will see God's salvation.'" (Luke 3:2–6) (emphasis added).

The voice was John's, but the one calling was the Spirit of the Lord. So it is for us today. If we will separate, the Spirit of the Lord will fill us with declarations of His second coming. The Spirit is seeking voices to cry through. He will embolden us to go into every place the Lord sends us to call people to forsake their sins and worldly pursuits, open their hearts to receive Jesus Christ as their Savior, and prepare for His imminent return. The glory of the Lord is about to be revealed throughout the world in unprecedented ways. Salvation is about to come to a billion souls.

Separation precedes crying out for repentance. Repentance precedes revival. Revival precedes an outpouring of the Holy Spirit to bring in the last harvest.

The last harvest precedes Jesus's second coming. Separate, saints! We are the John the Baptists for this generation.

8. *Separation Marks Us with* **Identification**.

In Exodus 11, we read that God's people were separated at Passover, each family in their own house. They were commanded to remove all the yeast from their houses, eat a roasted lamb, and put the blood of a lamb upon their doorposts. The blood was a sign identifying them as God's separated people, protecting them from the judgments to come. Exodus 12:12–13 (emphasis added) explains it for us: "…-and I will bring judgment on all the gods of Egypt. I am the Lord. The blood will be a sign for you on the houses where you are; and when I see the blood, *I will pass over you.* No destructive plague will touch you when I strike Egypt."

We are God's people, separated from the world and marked by His blood. His blood is the mark of our identity. He is our Lord. Partaking of Jesus, the Lamb of God, His roasted, crucified body becomes our food, and His blood becomes our life. We are CHRIST-ians, followers of the Lamb. We are separated from all the false gods of this world and marked by His blood. He will pass over us when He comes to judge the nations of the world. In frequent times of identification separation, we renew our communion with the Lord by partaking of His body and blood. I suggest taking frequent communion. It is important to take extended times of examination and meditation on the Lamb of God, His blood, and the Cross. In this sanctified separation, we take time to examine ourselves to purge all the yeast of sin and any fellowship with the gods of this world. We must be careful not to partake of the Lord's Supper in a religious, impersonal manner, leaving us vulnerable to sickness and death (see 1 Cor. 11:23–32).

Separation for identification marks us as blood-bought believers in Jesus. When plagues, wars, and destruction come upon the earth, the judgments of the Lord will pass over us. Separate yourself to plead His blood over you and your family.

9. *Separation Positions Us for **Impartation**.*

On Pentecost God imparted His Holy Spirit to separated disciples. In Acts 1:4 (emphasis added), Jesus said *"Do not leave* Jerusalem, but *wait* for the gift my Father promised,…" In verse 13, we read that "…they [separated themselves, coming out of their individual houses] went upstairs to the room,…" where verse 14 says, "They all *joined together* constantly in *prayer,…*" (emphasis added). Then Peter stood up to bring *apostolic order:* "May another take his [Judas] place of leadership" (v. 20).

Then, in Acts 2:1–4, we read:

> "When the day of Pentecost came, they were all together in one place. Suddenly a sound like the blowing of a violent wind came from heaven and filled the whole house where they were sitting. They saw what seemed to be tongues of fire that separated and came to rest on each of them. All of them were filled with the Holy Spirit

and began to speak in other tongues as the Spirit enabled them."

As He did in Acts, the Lord is commanding us today to separate for greater impartation, anointing, and power from the Holy Spirit. The time is now to go into our upper room and follow the protocol the Lord has set. First, we must not leave Jerusalem, attempting to do ministry without the Holy Spirit. We cannot go into the world with anything less than the presence and power of the Lord. Second, we must wait, positioning ourselves for the coming of the promise of the Father in a new and powerful way.

Third, we must become one. Unity is nonnegotiable. Unity will come when Jesus is the one and only focus of our hearts and wills. In Psalm 133, we see that unity in the body of Christ is the precedent condition for an outpouring of the Holy Spirit for a marriage, ministry, church, city, or nation. While there are many local expressions, there is only one church in our city or region. He will not come into an environment of religious legalism or performance, jealousy, division, competition, politics, unforgiveness, and so forth. Relational reconciliation must take place.

Fourth, separation for impartation will bring us to a place of passionate prayer. Individually and collectively, we will hunger and thirst for His presence and power; we will "pant hard" together as they did in the upper room, crying out and importuning the Lord until we fuse together in one passionate desire for the fulfillment of the Father's promise. We will stay and pray until we experience a fresh wind and fire of the Holy Spirit. Nothing short of this experience will equip us to go into the world to preach His gospel with signs following. Prayer meetings of all sizes, virtual and live, are taking place throughout the world. A call for the church to unite in prayer is going forth. Let's participate in every opportunity to pray.

Last of all, we must do what Peter did in the upper room: set our house in order. The kingdom order of authority in our individual lives, marriages, families, and churches must be established for the Holy Spirit to fill and reside in us. Our cities, regions, nations, and world will see an outpouring of the Holy Spirit and an ingathering of multitudes when kingdom order is in place. Then "suddenly" the Holy Spirit will be poured out in an unprecedented display of God's power and authority. His kingdom will come, and Jesus will be exalted as King. If we separate for impartation, we will not be disappointed. God will answer with fire when He finds a people who are hungry and thirsty for His presence, united in prayer and in kingdom order.

10. *Separation Releases* **Evangelization.**

Following the separation of the disciples in the upper room that produced an outpouring of the Holy Spirit on Pentecost, there was an explosion of evangelism. The empowered preaching of the gospel of Jesus Christ resulted in a huge ingathering of souls. Act 2:14–21 says, "Then Peter stood up with the Eleven, raised his voice and addressed the crowd:... 'In the last days, God says, I will pour out my Spirit on all people.... I will show wonders in the heavens above and signs on the earth below,... And everyone who calls on the name of the Lord will be saved.'" He then preached the uncompromising word of God in verses 40–41: "With many other words he warned them; and he pleaded with them, 'Save yourselves from this corrupt generation.' Those who accepted his message were baptized, and about three thousand were added to their number that day."

FINALLY

We are in the last days. The Spirit of God is about to be poured out on all people. A billion-soul ingathering is about to take place. All who have separated unto the Lord to allow Him to process them for His purposes will emerge as good-news carriers to demonstrate the signs and wonders of the Holy Spirit. With the fire of His love for His lost sons and daughters, we will stand and preach the pure, simple, and uncompromising gospel of our Lord Jesus. The Body of Christ will experience the joy of His manifest presence as multitudes are swept into His kingdom. These are the last and greatest days of the world.

Moses said to them, "It is the bread the Lord has given you to eat. This is what the Lord has commanded: 'each one is to gather as much as he needs...' The Israelites did as they were told: some gathered much, some little. (Exod. 16:15–17)

Jesus said to them, "I tell you the truth, it is not Moses who has given you the bread from heaven, but it is my Father who gives you the true bread from heaven. For the bread of God is he who comes down from heaven and gives life to the world."
"Sir," they said, "from now on give us this bread."
Then Jesus declared, "I am the bread of life. He who comes to me will never go hungry, and he who believes in me will never be thirsty."
(John 6: 32–35)

He told the crowd to sit down on the ground. Then he took the seven loaves and the fish, and when he had given thanks, he broke them and gave them to the disciples, and they in turn to the people. They all ate and were satisfied. Afterwards the disciples picked up seven basketfuls of broken pieces that were left over. (Matt. 15:35–37)

You prepare a table before me in the presence of my enemies.
You anoint my head with oil;
my cup overflows. (Ps. 23:5)

Chapter Five

Well-Done Christian Nuggets: Fast Food for Christians on the Run to Becoming Well-Done

Quick Principles and Prayers

While we are in the continuing process of becoming well-done, it is important to regularly dine at the table of the Lord. Engaging in frequent times of intimacy and strategic times of separation, dwelling in His presence, feasting on His Word, being still and listening for His voice, along with abundant praising, praying, and worshiping are all important keys in the process of becoming a well-done lover of God.

In between our main meals with the Lord, it is helpful to take some fast food to refresh our strength by activating the truths we've learned on our journey and adding a quick prayer to the Lord. These are some of my well-done Christian nuggets to chew on:

- It's not what I've done, but who I've become that pleases the Lord the most. *Lord, I surrender to being transformed by You.*

- The Great Commandment and the second commandment that follows supersede the Great Commission. *Lord, You are my first and only love. Grace me to love others with Your love and bring Your gospel of love to the world.*

- Performance will never produce His presence and power. *I surrender my self-sufficiency to You, Jesus. I need Your presence and power.*

- Busyness is the greatest diversion from intimacy. *I will still myself and spend quality time with You first. I trust You, Jesus, with all the demands on my life.*

- Communion ("common-union") is based on and begins with "communication." *Holy Spirit, help me to open my heart to Jesus and listen for His still, small voice.*

- If I want to possess something I've never had, I must do something I've never done. To do something I've never done, I must become someone I've never been. *Transform me, Lord, and work through me from the inside out.*

- God makes all things work together to bring me from crisis to Christlikeness, from pain to perfection. *Lord, I trust You completely with all I am walking through.*

- My level of joy is the litmus test for how much I am experiencing His presence and enjoying His pleasures. *Submerge me, Lord, in Your unspeakable joy, and fill me with Your glory.*

- God is enough! If God is not enough, nothing and no one else ever will be. *Lord, You are my Jehovah Jireh, my El Shaddai, my Provider and More than Enough.*

- Every new day begins in the dark. *Your word is a lamp unto my feet and a light unto my path.*

- Fear of the Lord destroys the fear of man. *Lord, I am in awe of You. What can man do to me? If God be for me, who can be against me?*

- In times of change, I will hold on to what never changes. *Lord, You are my rock. You are faithful and unchanging in all Your attributes, the same yesterday, today, and forever.*

- When the Lord gives me a work that's impossible, it's an opportunity to see the Lord work. *I declare that with God all things are possible.*

Now cook up your own well-done nuggets. Identify some of the key principles you have been learning during your journey to becoming a well-done lover of God. Write them in a succinct sentence and add a prayer to them. Strengthen yourself on them anytime you need a boost of quick energy. Chew on the principle, release the prayer, and enjoy the presence of God.

More Nuggets for the Hungry

- Knowing the Word by memorization is only information if there is no revelation and application. *Lord, open my eyes to see and my heart to receive your living Word.*

- Genuine revelation brings transformation, while information produces regulations. Regulations form religion, which results in condemnation. *Thank You, Lord, for converting me by your love into a new creation free from performance, guilt and shame.*

- When I agree with my old dead identity, I collapse into dysfunctionality; when I agree with my new re-created identity, I rise to my destiny. *Thank You, Father, that, as your loved child, You have great plans for me.*

- The longer I wait on the Lord, the shorter my deliverance takes. *As I wait upon You, Lord, I rise up as an eagle to run and not be weary, to walk and not faint.*

- The greatest joy does not come from seeing God work, but just from seeing God. *Open my eyes, Lord, to see Your glory.*

- The "suddenlies" of the Lord often take a long time to arrive. *I am "pre-prayering" myself for a visitation from You and am confident that You will come at just the right time.*

- Don't hesitate—communicate! *I will not allow the sun to go down on my anger, not miss an opportunity to go to a brother to be reconciled.*

- The more I see the great I Am, the more I see who I am. *Spirit of the Lord, reveal who You are that I may see You and be transformed into Your image from glory to glory.*

- Being born again is not a ritual—it's a revolution; it's not a religion—it's a re-formation. *I declare I am a new creation in Christ Jesus; the old is gone and the new has come.*

- When the enemy injects pictures into my mind, I will change the channel and gaze upon the Lord.

I will take every thought captive, making my thoughts obedient to the truth of God's Word.

- God is more concerned with my conformity to Christ than with my comfort. *Jesus, I thank you for and embrace the process You have me in despite the pain.*

- With regard to the voice of the Spirit, the Lord wants me to be not only a receiver, but also a transmitter. *Let me hear what the Spirit is saying. Then use me, Lord, as a trumpet, a John the Baptist, of Your love, mercies, and soon coming.*

- I often want the Lord to change my circumstances, but He wants to change me *in* my circumstances. *I yield to the Potter's hands that are molding me in every circumstance, knowing that He works all things together for my good and His glory.*

- Wrestling with God is good; resting in God is better. *I confess that in repentance and rest is my salvation.*

- Trials and tribulations can bring me into a higher place of torment or a deeper place of trust. *I will trust in the Lord with all my heart. I will not lean on my own understanding but will acknowledge Him in all things, and He will make my path straight.*

- If everything I have is gone and all I have is the Lord, I have everything I will ever need or want. *Lord, You are my all-in-all and my exceedingly great reward.*

- Transition that brings character transformation begins at the point where I acknowledge that I am not enough to meet the challenge of where I am going. *Holy Spirit, I need You. Lead me, strengthen me, and change me to be the person I need to be to fulfill my destiny.*

- What bound me in the past is the object of His purging in the present to free me to come into His purposes in the future. *Search me, oh Lord, and see if there be any wickedness or wound in me. Heal me and make me whole.*

- When I see how great the Lord is, I see how small my problems are. *Let me see Your awesome glory in my secret place, as David did, that I might be able to speak to my Goliath with authority and power.*

- An exalted view of God brings a clear view of sin and a realistic view of self. *Open my eyes, as You did for Isaiah, to see You high and lifted up, surrounded by all of heaven crying, "Holy, holy, holy is the Lord God Almighty." Cause me to experience the ongoing cleansing of Your blood that enables me to stand in Your presence.*

- Focus is the faculty of the heart that facilitates fruit. *Holy Spirit, give me singular vision to keep my eyes on Jesus, the beginning and end of all I will become.*

- Nothing activates changes in me more than changes outside me. *Give me grace, Lord, to be able to say like Joseph: You meant it for evil, but God used it to change me and meant it for good for the salvation of many.*

- Nothing crucifies like a crisis. God will use a crisis to transform me into the image of Christ. *Grace me, Lord, to say in every trying situation, "Not my will but Yours be done."*

- Christ often uses things I don't like to make me more Christlike. *Lord, when they take my cloak, grant me the love to give them my coat and go the second mile.*

- To get something I don't have, I must often give something I do have. I grow when I sow. *All I have* and all I am belong to You, Jesus. *Teach me to be a lavish lover and generous giver.* As the martyr Jim Elliot said, "He is no fool who gives what he cannot keep to gain what he cannot lose."

- God's blessings are spiritual before they become material. *Train me, Lord, in the gift of faith so that what I see and say according to your will becomes reality.*

- A gift is a transaction of giving and receiving. *Train me in the Spirit, Lord, to give to You all that I am so that I might receive all that You are.*

- The Lord becomes all I need when He becomes all I want. *More than anything, Jesus, I want who You are, not what You can do for me.*

- I wouldn't be who I am today if the Lord hadn't saved me from all my yesterdays. *I praise You, Jesus. You are my deliverer and healer.*

- Am I waiting on the Lord or telling Him to wait? *Lord, here I am. Send me.*

- Too often, other people can't hear what I am saying because who I am is shouting. *Transform me, Lord, so that what I say is validated by who I am and opens the hearts of people You want to reach.*

- The purity of my heart determines the power of my prayers. *Purge all hidden motives and unrenewed thinking, Lord, so that my prayers are initiated by the Holy Spirit and in line with Your perfect will.*

- Praise is the power to prevail. *I will praise You, Jesus, in the midst of the battle.*

- My life is Christ's, and Christ's life is mine. His life is in me, and my life is in Him. *I praise and thank the Lord that Christ is in me, the hope of glory, and that I am seated in Him in heavenly places.*

A Recipe for Fried Christian

- People learn little from success, but much from failure. *Thank You, Lord, that you have used every one of my failures to reveal Yourself in new ways, to strengthen and transform me.*

- Don't listen to yourself; talk to yourself. *I prophesy specific promises of God to be fulfilled in my life.*

- How do I live in resurrected life? First, I must die. How do I die? People and circumstances crucify me. I must then surrender to the Father like Jesus did, resting and trusting the Father as I go through the dying process. The Father will then faithfully resurrect me in Christ to overcoming life. *Father, in every situation, I trust You in the process of death, burial, and resurrection, knowing that You are faithful to bring me forth transformed and victorious in Christ.*

- Gaze at the Lord, glance at problems. *You are my good, good Father. I will keep my eyes on You. I am convinced nothing can separate me from Your love.*

- Quickly move from problem mode, to praise mode, to prayer mode. *Holy Spirit, take over as I walk through various valleys. Keep my heart free from fear and assured that no weapon formed against me will prosper, and no evil will come near my tent. I will feast at the table You have prepared before me in the presence of my enemies.*

- Rest, refresh, replenish, repeat. *I will come away to be with my Lord daily, for special retreats, and at strategic times.*

- Don't make much of anything; make much of the Lord. Don't magnify problems; magnify His goodness. Don't lift up anything above His Word and name. He doesn't want to be first; He wants to be the only. *Jesus, You are my sovereign, my king, my Lord, my lover, the "one thing" of my life.*

- Settle it: God is everything He says He is. *I exalt you as King of kings and Lord of lords. You are the great "I Am."*

- Responsibility is my response and His ability. *I can do all things through Christ who strengthens me. When I am weak, He is strong.*

- I have been converted from living from the outside in to living from the inside out. *Teach me, Lord, how to live and walk by the Spirit and not by the flesh.*

Forget the former things;
do not dwell on the past.
See, I am doing a new thing!
Now it springs up; do you not perceive it?
I am making a way in the desert
and streams in the wasteland.
(Isa. 43:18-19)

Jesus went through all the towns and villages, teaching in their synagogues, preaching the good news of the kingdom and healing every disease and sickness. When he saw the crowds, he had compassion on them, because they were harassed and helpless, like sheep without a shepherd. Then he said to his disciples, "The harvest is plentiful but the workers are few. Ask the Lord of the harvest, therefore, to send out workers into his harvest field." (Matt. 9:35–38)

As you go, preach this message: the kingdom of heaven is near. Heal the sick, raise the dead, cleanse those who have leprosy, drive out demons. Freely you have received, freely give. (Matt. 10:7–8)

Chapter Six

Well-Done Christian Cordon Bleu: Serving the Best to a Hungry World

THE END PURPOSES OF THE FATHER

In bringing us through the transformation process, the Father wants to accomplish the following:

> *To conform us to the image of Jesus,*
> *Merge us into a love union with the Father and the Son,*
> *Causing us to become a tangible expression of His love,*
> *So the world will believe in Jesus.*

SERVING OURSELVES TO THE WORLD

Hungry people consume fruit because it is attractive, promises to taste good and nourish them. In like manner, hungry people come to Christ-followers whose characters and lives attract them. They will consume our time, our love, our gifts, and our very life. What they are looking for, desperately need, and hopefully will receive is the life and love of Christ in us. The Father does not want the world to be served fried Christians, who are burned out, bitter, toxic, and look and taste like rotten fruit. We are to live out the message of His love in the character of Christ and the fruit of His Spirit. The Lord wants hungry people to be served the best! As I like to say, we are to serve ourselves as "Well-Done Christian Cordon Bleu".

TESTIMONIES OF HIS TRANSFORMING POWER

Along our journey to becoming a completely well-done lover of God, the Lord will have us give out what He has already put in. These servings test our fruit, bless others, and produce a testimony of the good work He has already done in transforming us, which brings Him glory and encourages us to continue in the process. Here are a couple of my "well-done Christian cordon bleu" testimonies.

Testimony 1: From Tragedy to Triumph

When Jackie and I decided to move from New York we wanted to live close to our family. While we had the option to move to Florida to be close to either of our other two daughters, their husbands, and our nine grandchildren there, we felt directed by the Lord to move to Houston to be close to our youngest daughter, husband, and three grandchildren in Houston. For a year and a half after we moved, the questions in the back of my mind were, *Why are we here?* and *What do we do with the rest of our life?* Having no home church and no ministry, coupled with the processes I had been through, helped me to conquer my works mentality, rest and enjoy this unique time with the family. Life was good.

Then suddenly, tragedy hit. Our then twelve-year-old grandson, Luc, collapsed in school, was rushed to the hospital, and airlifted to the medical center in the city. He had suffered a massive stroke and was immediately brought into surgery. The testimony of the surgeon was that Luc had been within seconds of dying. Considering the many possible delays and detours that could have happened from his collapse in school—time to the ambulance, to the hospital, to the life flight, to the immediate need for a surgeon, to the extremely dangerous surgery—it was nothing short of many miracles that saved his life that day. For almost three months, my daughter and son-in-love lived in the hospital as Luc endured four more surgeries. His entire left side was paralyzed. Jackie and I covered the bases at home, taking care of the other two children and providing transportation in and out of the city for extended family flying into town—and prayer, prayer, prayer. It was obvious now why the Lord had led us to move to Houston.

The challenges through all this for our entire family were enormous, including the shock, physical and emotional exhaustion, so many fears for Luc, the "WHY" questions, and our collective faith under assault. As I personally walked through this time I realized that the processes the Lord brought me through strengthened me to pray, serve, bring comfort to others and continue to believe that my good Father would continue to work on Luc's behalf and for his good.

Almost 4 years later, while we continue to believe for a full recovery of Luc's left side, he is growing into a tall, strong, very intelligent young man who is overcoming obstacles with courage, perseverance and a winning attitude. He is an encourager to everyone he meets especially those at his therapy centers. His favorite question is "Are you loving life?" He is an inspiration to all of us. I am convinced the Lord has a great plan and destiny for Luc that will not be denied him.

Testimony 2: From Retired to Refired

When we moved from New York to Texas, we left all ministry responsibilities behind. I knew that if the Lord were ever to use me again, He would have to raise up something brand-new. Even though I had the opportunity to retire, the concept didn't fit the many prophecies I had received over the years and the desire of my heart to "leave it all on the field." However, there was nothing for me to do but to wait upon the Lord.

I had learned enough to know that I should not attempt to go out before I was sent. Trying to develop something in my own strength would violate everything I had learned. I was compelled to wait, and allow some of the processes I was in to continue. The Lord was reviewing what I had learned, testing my heart to see if I had reached various degrees of completion and if I was convinced in who I was in Him. He continued to correct, adjust, and refine my character. While the "tragedy to triumph" testimony I shared above was taking place, the Lord was also beginning to do a new thing. After we had lived with our daughter, son-in-love, and three grandchildren for almost five months, the Lord found my wife and me a perfect little house. Two weeks after moving in, we received an envelope from a former student of mine. Within it was the brochure for a ministry called Harvest Now, founded by Guine and Lisa Anderson.

Lisa had been one of my primo students at Christ for the Nations. We sent her to Hong Kong for her internship study, where she met a young man, Guine Anderson, a missionary from Texas. They married and formed a missions organization that now supports hundreds of pastors, churches, and orphanages in India, China, and the Far East. The brochure listed their missions address in Houston. I looked it up and discovered that, with 4.5 million people in Houston, they lived only seven houses from us around the corner. What are the chances!

The Lord reunited us, and after the "triumph to tragedy" testimony, He opened up opportunities for my wife and I to minister with them to the underground church in China, Hong Kong, and the Far East. On a trip to Myanmar, I was privileged to preach the gospel to an unreached Buddhist village living by a garbage dump. Love for them filled my heart. I knew it was the love the Lord had put there through all the processes I had gone through. The entire village received Jesus as their Lord and Savior, with the chief receiving a healing of a heart condition. That's what I call well-done Christian cordon bleu. Years earlier, I could only have served them fried Christian, but now the personal, tangible love of God delivered by a transformed son of God converted them from dead religion and demonic oppression into a love relationship with Jesus.

But the testimony does not end there. After more than two years in Houston we still didn't have a church home, so Lisa brought Jackie and I to Dwelling Place Church in Houston. DPC has a vision to bring the presence and love of God to the world. The message and ministry of the church perfectly complemented and enhanced all the processes I had been in, and Jackie and I were immediately received. One of their mottos is "Find your home, find your destiny." The Lord led us to our new home there and reopened our destiny. We've since traveled with them to the nations and are serving in multiple church ministries. Even more, the Lord released us to launch Dennis and Jackie Bambino Ministries, sending us out to minister nationally and internationally.

The Lord never planned for me to retire. However, it was necessary that I continue processing in order to reach a certain level of maturity before He would release me to go forward into His plans and purposes. That's a good, good Father caring for me and all those He would send me to. Instead of serving fried Christian, I can now serve well-done Christian cordon bleu.

> *Well done lovers of God don't retire, they get continually refired.*

> Now when Joshua was near Jericho, he looked up and saw a man standing in front of him with a drawn sword in his hand. Joshua went up to him and asked, "Are you for us or for our enemies?"
> "Neither," he replied, "but as commander of the army of the Lord I have now come." Then Joshua fell face down to the ground in reverence, and asked him, "What message does my Lord have for his servant?"
> The commander of the Lord's army replied, "Take off your sandals, for the place where you are standing is holy." And Joshua did so. (Josh. 5:13–15).

I have fought the good fight, I have finished the race, I have kept the faith. Now there is in store for me the crown of righteousness, which the Lord, the righteous Judge, will award to me on that day—and not only to me, but also to all who have longed for his appearing. (2 Tim. 4:7–8)

Do you not know that in a race all the runners run, but only one gets the prize? Run in such a way as to get the prize. Everyone who competes in the games goes into strict training. They do it to get a crown that will not last; but we do it to get a crown that will last forever. (1 Cor. 9:24–25)

Chapter Seven

An Invitation to Become a Well-Done Lover of God

HELP! I'M FRIED!

Don't despair. I've been there—in darkness and despair—spiritually emotionally, mentally, and physically burned out. In His faithfulness, the Lord intervened, caught me in my free fall into darkness, and delivered me into a love relationship with Him. This same God, who revealed Himself to me as my loving Father and compassionate Savior, loves you and is present right now to deliver you from destruction into His marvelous plan. Jeremiah 29:11–14 says:

> "For I know the plans I have for you," declares the Lord, "plans to prosper you and not to harm you, plans to give you hope and a future. Then you will call upon me and come and pray to me, and I will listen to you. You will seek me and find me when you seek me with all of your heart.

I will be found by you," declares the Lord, "and will bring you back from captivity."

The Father whose love I've come to know personally loves you also with the same extraordinary love He has for Jesus. As His love transformed me, He will also bring you from darkness into light, from hurt into healing, from destruction into destiny, from pressure to perform into peace, and from dead religion into a living, loving relationship with Him. He is ready right now to take what the enemy meant for evil in your life and turn it into good. He will give you new purpose for your life and revive your destiny.

He will align you with His plan for you:

- To be transformed into the image of Jesus;
- To be merged into a love union with Jesus and the Father; and
- To become a tangible expression of the Father's love so the world will believe in Jesus.

This is a personal invitation from the Lord calling you to surrender, to separate, to serve, and to stand.

To Surrender

At one point in my free fall into darkness, I became fearful that I would never return. The Lord waited until I was totally spent, with nothing left in me to try to save myself. At that point, He gave me the grace to quit striving, tap out of the struggle, resign all my responsibilities, and surrender to Him.

If you've come to the end of yourself as I did, don't wait another minute. Don't stay in the frying process one second longer. It's time, right now, to go before the Lord with all your heart and quit, tap out, resign, and surrender to Him. Bow your head in complete humility before Him, raise both your hands into the air as a sign of absolute surrender, and put your whole heart on the altar before Him. Give the Lord full permission to bring you through all the processes necessary to take you from fried to well-done. When I did that, it was amazing to discover that the Lord was there the whole time, waiting for me to surrender. Do it now! He's there, waiting to heal you, transform you into His image as a well-done lover of God, and refire you destiny.

To Separate

Immediately after my surrender to the Lord, He separated me from everything else and began developing a one-on-one, first-love relationship with Him. During many precious times, He revealed His character and His love for me. He healed my past and began writing the second part of my story.

In the same way, He is calling you to come away with Him, where in intimate times, He will have you revisit (preferably, write out) the first part of your story, with all its pain and its pleasures. In great detail, the Lord will walk with you through all your dreams and visions, your journey, all that happened to you, and how it made you feel. The Holy Spirit will reveal all the ingredients that went into your becoming fried and that led you into your dark night of the soul. In precious times together, the Lord will reveal Himself to you in a way you have never known Him before. He will woo you into a first-love relationship with Him. Along the way, He will lead you through the processes and take you to the places that transform you into His very image and likeness. You will begin the exciting adventure of being changed by the Spirit from the inside out as He starts to write the second part of your story. Ready? Set. Separate!

To Serve

As my journey progressed with the Lord, I continued by His grace to surrender and separate. This allowed Him to do many more wonderful things in my character, continually filling me with His love and transforming me into His image. Although I am not completely well-done, He has invited me to give out what He has already put in. He has called me to serve the best of who He is in me to "the least of these" I encounter in the world.

In the same way, having surrendered and separated, He will invite you to join Him in seeking and saving those who are lost and fried. He will want you to tell them your story, how He redeemed you, how much they are loved, and that they too can be healed and made whole. He will serve you as a well-done demonstration of who He is—love.

To Stand

While I have not yet experienced this, I am convinced the day will come when each of His well-done lovers of God will have finished their race, completed their processes, fought the good fight, and kept the faith. You will be among them. You will stand before the Lord unashamed and without regret, and you will receive the rewards He has stored up for you. Then, as He places crowns on your head that you will cast at his feet, with tears of joy streaming down your face, you will hear the sweet voice of your lover and Lord say to you:

> "Well done, good and faithful servant! You have been faithful with a few things; I will put you in charge of many things. Come and share your master's happiness!"

Closing Prayer

Thank You, Jesus, for Your faithful, wise, and compassionate love that continues to transform me into Your image, a well-done lover of God. Use me as a living testimony of Your transforming power to a world that desperately needs a Savior.

Father, I have experienced Your faithful love. What you have done for me, you will do for all Your sons and daughters. I therefore pray for my brothers and sisters who have gone through horrific experiences in life that have left them in various degrees of being burned out. Father, reveal to them how much You love them and that You have sent Your Son to heal them and bring them into a love relationship with You and Jesus. Catch them as You did me, I pray, in their free fall into darkness, and carry them into a safe place in You.

In the security of Your love, heal and transform them. Give them the grace to continually surrender to all the processes You will bring them through to conform them to Your image. Separate them from the world, and bring them into an abiding love relationship with Jesus. Bind up their broken heart, comfort them in their distress, remove all their fears and wipe away all their tears. Holy Spirit, remove the orphan spirit and impart to them the spirit of sonship. Lord, give them a crown of beauty instead of ashes, the oil of joy instead of mourning, and a garment of praise for a spirit of despair. Deliver them, as You have delivered me, from spiritual burnout, and transform them into a well-done lover of God. Use them as a living demonstration of Your extraordinary love for the world.

Jesus, receive all the glory, honor, thanksgiving, and praise for all You are, all You have done, all You are doing, and all that is yet to come. Everything you do, Lord, is well done.

In Jesus's precious name, amen.

About The Author

Dennis Bambino answered the call to full-time ministry while hiking the Swiss Alps in 1984. Shortly thereafter, he resigned his position as a successful corporate executive and enrolled full-time in Bible school. Since then, Dennis has served the Lord in various capacities, including senior pastor, Director of Student Ministries at Christ for the Nations Long Island, and member of the Apostolic Council of Christ Covenant Coalition. Additionally, Dennis is a church planter, founder of a regional Bible school, and co-founder of a regional prayer network and regional evangelistic initiatives.

A prophetic teacher to the Body of Christ, he is considered a revivalist calling the Church to fulfill Ephesians 4:11-16.

Together with Jackie, his wife of 53 years, they have ministered nationally and internationally in over 30 countries at churches, retreats, conferences, and crusades.

With a heart to see believers mature in their faith, they equip the Body of Christ through preaching and teaching from the Word, facilitating the healing ministry of the Holy Spirit, and hands-on leadership training.

A Certified Public Accountant, Dennis holds a business degree from St. John's University and is also credentialed as a Life Forming Leadership coach. Drawing from his extensive experience in business and ministry, he is a consultant to churches for strategic planning and leadership development.

Residing in Houston, Texas, Dennis and Jackie have three happily married daughters, 12 grandchildren and a Shih-Tzu named Pebbles. In his leisure time, he enjoys spending time with his grandchildren and playing tennis.

To contact Dennis, go to:

<u>WWW.DJBAMBINOMINISTRIES.ORG</u>
DENNIS@DJBAMBINOMINISTRIES.ORG

CPSIA information can be obtained
at www.ICGtesting.com
Printed in the USA
LVHW022107280521
688850LV00008B/505